TO THINK IS TO SAY NO

To Think Is to Say No

Jacques Derrida

EDITED BY BRIEUC GÉRARD

TRANSLATED BY PASCALE-ANNE BRAULT AND MICHAEL NAAS

FORDHAM UNIVERSITY PRESS NEW YORK 2026

Ouvrage publié avec le concours du Ministère français chargé de la Culture–Centre National du Livre.

This work has been published with the assistance of the French Ministry of Culture–National Center for the Book.

This book was originally published in French as *Penser, c'est dire non*. Copyright © Éditions du Seuil, 2022.

Fordham University Press also publishes its books in a variety of electronic formats. Some content that appears in print may not be available in electronic books.

Visit us online at www.fordhampress.com.

For EU safety / GPSR concerns: Mare Nostrum Group B.V., Doelen 72, 4831 GR Breda, The Netherlands, gpsr@mare-nostrum.co.uk

Library of Congress Cataloging-in-Publication Data available online at https://catalog.loc.gov.

Printed in the United States of America

28 27 26 5 4 3 2 1

First edition

Contents

Preface: *Yes No*

Brieuc Gérard

The lecture course "To Think Is to Say No" was given by Jacques Derrida at the Sorbonne during the 1960–1961 academic year. For four years Derrida served as an assistant in philosophy and logic to professors such as Georges Canguilhem, Suzanne Bachelard, Jean Wahl, and Paul Ricoeur. As he recalls in a tribute to Ricoeur published in the *Cahiers de L'Herne*,[1] he was given complete freedom in determining the topics of his courses and the organization of smaller discussion groups. This would change in 1964 when Derrida moved to the École Normale Supérieure, where he was required each year to follow the philosophy *agrégation* program. Despite a considerable workload, Derrida described his years at the Sorbonne as the happiest of his teaching career.[2] The writings that came out of this teaching, most still unpublished to this day, covered a wide range of topics.[3]

It is in this context that Derrida devoted four teaching sessions to Alain's phrase, which also serves as the title of this

1. Jacques Derrida, "La parole—Donner, nommer, appeler," in *Paul Ricoeur: Cahiers de L'Herne* (Paris: L'Herne, 2004), 21.

2. Jacques Derrida, "Discours de réception de la Légion d'honneur," unpublished, IMEC archives, call number 219DRR/253/5,1992.

3. [Two courses on Husserl, both given in the spring of 1963, the first on the notion of God, titled "Phenomenology. Theology. Teleology. Husserl's God," and the second on the fifth of Husserl's *Cartesian Meditations*, have recently been published as *Du même à l'autre: Deux cours sur Husserl*, ed. Edouard Mehl and Raphaël Authier (Paris: Seuil, 2024)—Trans.]

work. Without specific dates, it is difficult to know exactly when this course took place during the year. There is, however, one material element that locates the course within a rather specific time period. The manuscript is written on paper with the header "Faculty of Letters and Social Sciences. History of Colonization,"[4] a reminder that the course coincides with a turbulent period in Derrida's native Algeria, which gained its independence the following year, in 1962. This same letterhead was also used by Derrida for his introduction to Edmund Husserl's *The Origin of Geometry*, which he translated and completed in July 1961.

The text of *To Think Is to Say No*, handwritten by Derrida for a lecture course, was never intended for publication and has remained unpublished until now. Yet it now becomes the very first text of the Derridean corpus, the first text published *by* Derrida, "Force and Signification,"[5] appearing in 1963.

* * *

"Yes" and "no," two fundamental "little words" in Derridean thought, are central to Derrida's writings of the 1960s, a decade of intense intellectual activity in France. During this time Derrida returned frequently to the differences in this pair of words and the questions raised by it. The tension between these two words, if we can even call them that, since, as Derrida suggests elsewhere, we perhaps do not yet

4. The chair of colonial history at the Sorbonne was abolished in 1961. It was then held by the journalist and historian Charles-André Julien (1891–1991). See *La construction du discours colonial: L'empire français aux xix*e *et xx*e *siècles*, ed. Oissila Saaïdia and Laurick Zerbini (Paris: Karthala Éditions, 2009), 48.

5. Jacques Derrida, "Force et signification," *Critique* 193–194 (June–July 1963). Republished in *L'écriture et la différence* (Paris: Seuil, 1967); "Force and Signification," in *Writing and Difference*, trans. Alan Bass (Chicago: University of Chicago Press, 1978).

know what these little words mean or how they function in language,[6] is thus more than a fundamental mechanism of deconstruction. It also serves as an important pedagogical and rhetorical reference point for Derrida in his early teaching years. As early as 1959–1960, while teaching at the Lycée Montesquieu in Le Mans, Derrida asks not about saying no but about saying nothing by way of the question of the negativity of silence. In 1961–1962, while taking up another key question, "What Is Appearance?" Derrida makes reference to the same philosophers he appealed to in *To Think Is to Say No*, exploring another form of negativity, that of appearance. He returns again to the "no" in 1963–1964 in a lecture course on Bergson and the idea of nothingness, and in another titled "The Origin of Refutation," where he revisits the theme of negation and the origin of nothingness in Sartre. But he returns to it especially in 1962–1963, in a six-session lecture course titled "Can We Say Yes to Finitude?," where Derrida criticizes his students for being so fascinated by the term "finitude" in their essays that they neglected its intrinsic relation to the question of the "yes," the possibility of "saying yes," or no, to finitude. The critique of "saying," as a speech act, was also, of course, not absent during these years. In 1961–1962, in a course on "Intuition," Derrida says that a philosopher is "perhaps one who has heard a certain imperative of speech, that is to say, the duty to *speak* both to give meaning and to conform to meaning, and to establish through respect for meaning the duty of speech within a right to speech."[7]

Like many of his later seminars, but contrary to a cer-

6. Jacques Derrida, "Ulysses Gramophone: Hear Say Yes in Joyce," in *Acts of Literature*, ed. Derek Attridge, trans. Tina Kendall and Shari Benstock (New York: Routledge, 1992), 256.

7. Jacques Derrida, "L'intuition," unpublished, IMEC archives, 1961–1962, 2.

tain number of lecture courses from the same period, for which we have only scattered notes, *To Think Is to Say No* was fully written out by Derrida before being read to his students. Insertions, deletions, and corrections in different colored ink indicate a process of rereading and revision that Derrida would follow throughout his entire career. We also find Derrida's pedagogical practice of indicating moments of improvisation through didascalia (e.g., "Comment in detail"). This text also has the peculiarity of having been used by Derrida as a model for students to compare to their own essays. Derrida in fact writes at one point: "Too often in your essays you became fixated on the possible objects of negation, and you enumerated everything to which consciousness could say no." Another material peculiarity of this course is that it was entirely handwritten. Notoriously difficult to decipher, Derrida's handwriting posed a significant editorial challenge. There was no certainty at the beginning of this project that the manuscript that led to this publication could be deciphered in its entirety and its integrity maintained. A long process, spanning several years, involving various decoding strategies such as the software Scrabble, resulted in a database of more than 1,500 words written in Derrida's hand. Despite these efforts, some illegible words remain, words that have resisted the scrutiny of many pairs of seasoned and attentive eyes. These unresolved moments, which nowhere hinder reading and comprehension of the text, are marked in the text as "[illegible word]," the hope being that they will one day be deciphered.

This edition was based on digitized files of the original manuscript of the lecture course preserved in the Jacques Derrida Collection at the Critical Theory Archive of the University of California, Irvine,[8] and the Derrida Collection

8. The original manuscript is located in box 4, folder 16, of the Jacques Derrida collection.

at IMEC. The four sessions of the text comprise 109 handwritten pages, in addition to about twenty pages of notes and author quotations used in the course. These latter are included in an appendix at the end of the work. I have tried to maintain the original page layout as much as possible. Some manuscript marks (deletions, arrows, emphasis symbols, etc.) were omitted for the sake of clarity. When pertinent, they are included in footnotes. Readers can consult the originals through the Derrida Archive Project at Princeton University.[9]

* * *

To Think Is to Say No is primarily devoted to the deconstruction of a phrase by the philosopher Alain (1868–1951).[10] Through this provocative, even striking phrase, what interests Derrida is at the same time the radical conviction of the thought of Alain, a committed antifascist and pacifist. Alain's philosophy is characterized by a unique literary genre, "Propos," fragments of thought that are at once everyday reflections and sharp philosophical propositions. There are very few references to Alain in Derrida's corpus. *To Think Is to Say No* does refer, however, to many other authors whom Derrida would continue to read and reread. Although this text predates the foundational texts of what would come to be called "deconstruction," it is nothing less than a Derridean reading of Alain's phrase that is offered here. Derrida is keen to expose all the tension that animates this phrase and to play with the contradictions of what is said (and not said) when one says no, yes, and when one says that to think is to say no. Derrida seeks first to explain Alain's intentions and then to go beyond them. In so doing, he provides his

9. https://dpul.princeton.edu/derridaseminars.
10. [Alain was the pseudonym used by Émile-Auguste Chartier —Trans.]

students at the Sorbonne with an outline for a paper they had previously worked on. This manuscript thus serves as a model for them, as is evident when Derrida points out the mistakes students made in their assignments. We thus see here a methodological exercise with regard both to form, at the level of the pedagogical, and substance, through references to a wide range of logicians.

The yes no, far from being a simple binary pair, is presented as the fundamental, originary question of the act of thinking. For that is indeed the question at the outset of Derrida's course: what is thought? For Alain, what animates thought, what awakens it, is the search for rest, for adequation with itself and a certain reconciliation with the world through the search for a final affirmation, that of truth. In seeking to say yes, yes, this is that, thought would reach its final destination and thus would reach itself. It would then give up its search, giving itself over to slumber in the form of belief. Thought is therefore thought only in its journey toward truth. It is born in the movement that brings it to truth and thus in the power of negativity. That is why Alain says that to think is to say no. The apparent opposition of yes and no is thus surpassed by the question of origin and primacy; which comes first, the yes or the no? Derrida's analysis unfolds in three major stages. In the first, he follows Alain's assertion that all thought is *une conscience*, that is, at once consciousness and conscience. As such, it is first a moral duty to seek truth and reject appearances.

To say no to what? According to Derrida, this is a secondary, derivative question. The second stage goes beyond Alain's phrase and establishes the fundamental intransitivity of the no. The no is the constitutive project of consciousness, and rejection is its form. The object of negation is merely an appearance. In reality, thought says no to nothing other than itself for having believed in appearances, for having first said yes. Hence "to negate" is primarily "to negate oneself." "There is no other struggle in the world," says Alain, than that of thought negating itself. Derrida explains that before confronting the other, and in order to confront the other, I must confront the enemy within me (it is a Trojan War, for the enemy is always already there) that urges me to sleep, to believe in appearances without examination. If yes "indicates that there is address to the other,"[11] as Derrida notes in *Ulysses Gramophone*, no is first and always addressed to oneself. Whether it be no to the world, to the tyrant, to the preacher: three addressees, three figures, through which the mind is in dialogue with itself; three noes, all primarily and fundamentally noes to oneself.

Finally, the last and by far the longest stage is the one that brings about "a radical critique of belief in general." It is divided into three sections.

The first presents the philosophical presuppositions of Alain's phrase. Derrida locates Alain's radical critique of belief within a voluntarist philosophy of freedom and judgment. For Alain, belief is a naive attitude where, even if what I believe turns out to be true, my thought would be in error. Indeed, thought is thought only in a free movement towards the truth. On this point, Derrida (always already) true to himself does not miss the chance to question his own position as a teacher:

> That is why teaching is such a difficult thing. It would be easy—there would be nothing to it—if its task were simply to transmit the truth. It must also teach thought, which is something other than a technique of truth; and as soon as truth is tied to a

11. Derrida, "Ulysses Gramophone," 299.

> technique, well, one is already the victim of the two falsifications of thought, apparently distant from one another and even contradictory, but whose affinity no doubt runs deep: sophistry and dogmatism.

The great radicality of Alain's philosophy is revealed in the fact that the idea of proof as a technical instrument of truth is to be rejected, for as soon as one says yes, one stops thinking and begins to believe. One should constantly destroy proof as a reassuring and protective abode for truth. For Alain, truth must not be a treasure, a secret to be protected. It must not be fixed; it must be endlessly begun anew (38–39, 41). Derrida concludes that the ultraradicalism of Alain's doubt might have been disapproved of by his mentor, Descartes. Where the latter's methodical doubt would end in truth, Alain's is endless. And so Derrida claims that Alain would be more Cartesian than Descartes himself. Nevertheless, far from seeing here a simple repetition compulsion, Derrida defines this endless quest as a coming to awareness that doubt has an intrinsic value and is the very salvation of thought, rather than just its instrument. This allows us to read a moment of Derridean writing whose form will become typical of its author and will undoubtedly make his translators shudder:

> For Alain, what is proper to incredulity is that when it shows its measure it no longer has any measure. It is measureless, *immeasurable*, *immoderate*. And it is by the measure of this immeasurability that truth is measured. There is truth only by the measure of incredulity. This is what is expressed, in substance, by this text, where fidelity to the Cartesian spirit seems to me to be an infidelity to the spirit of Descartes.

To say no, one must will to do so, Derrida recalls. And this willing is the result of an affirmation, one that says yes to the value of truth and to the very will to truth. One must therefore believe before anything else. In other words, thought, in order to be sure of being thought, sure of being itself, says yes to itself before being able to say no.

In a second section, Derrida moves beyond Alain's phrase. Tracing the limits of Alain's reflection, Derrida here sets to work the mechanisms of a deconstructive writing to come where this "yes" says no, abandons its guise of credulous naivete to take on that of faith. Derrida notes in addition that to say yes is to take up speech and that this act of language breaks away from any credulous and preobjective belief in being. For Alain, if the no opens the space of axiology, the yes of faith establishes this same space. Derrida then undertakes a rigorous examination of the meaning and value of this axiological yes of faith.

Finally, the last section reveals the general significance of all these questions by leading the reader to the double question of the origin of negation and the anteriority of axiological affirmation. After a brief review of the history of negation, from Plato to Hegel, by way of Kant and a handful of logicians, Derrida focuses on the question of nothingness through Bergson in order to reaffirm, in particular, the impossible symmetry between the yes and the no. It is by confronting Husserl with Bergsonism that Derrida will demonstrate that even if the yes comes before the no, there is nevertheless always already a possible negation before judgment and before language. Granting Sartre one of the most nuanced analyses of the origin of negation, Derrida examines the criticisms Sartre levels at Husserl on this theme. This review concludes with a reference to Heidegger and to a certain ontic-ontological difference that "would allow us truly to understand Alain when he says that 'to think is to say no.'"

It quickly becomes apparent upon reading this text that Derrida first sees in Alain's phrase the chance to stage a doubleness whose difference exceeds that of a simple binary pair. The no is certainly not symmetrical to the yes, as Derrida reminds us elsewhere.[12] These two little words are perhaps closer to another pair on which Derrida would focus his attention a decade or so later, that of life/death, where Derrida also emphasizes the differentiality of this pair of words through a logic without opposition of *différance*. In addition to showing the marks of a deconstructive writing before the publication of its foundational texts, *To Think Is to Say No* also demonstrates that the thought of the "yes no" will have always been fundamental to Derrida's thinking. Its relevance perhaps takes on its full significance today, at a time when it is often difficult to see, or to say, the difference between thought and belief.

* * *

I would like to express my deep gratitude to all those who made the publication of this work possible. I am especially thankful to Katie Chenoweth for her invaluable help and advice throughout this process, to Geoffrey Bennington for his attentive suggestions, to Peggy Kamuf for her initial encouragement, and to François Bordes, who graciously responded to my inquiries. Above all, I am grateful to Pierre Alferi and Jean Derrida for their confidence and support of this project.

12. Derrida, "Ulysses Gramophone," 274.

TO THINK IS TO SAY NO

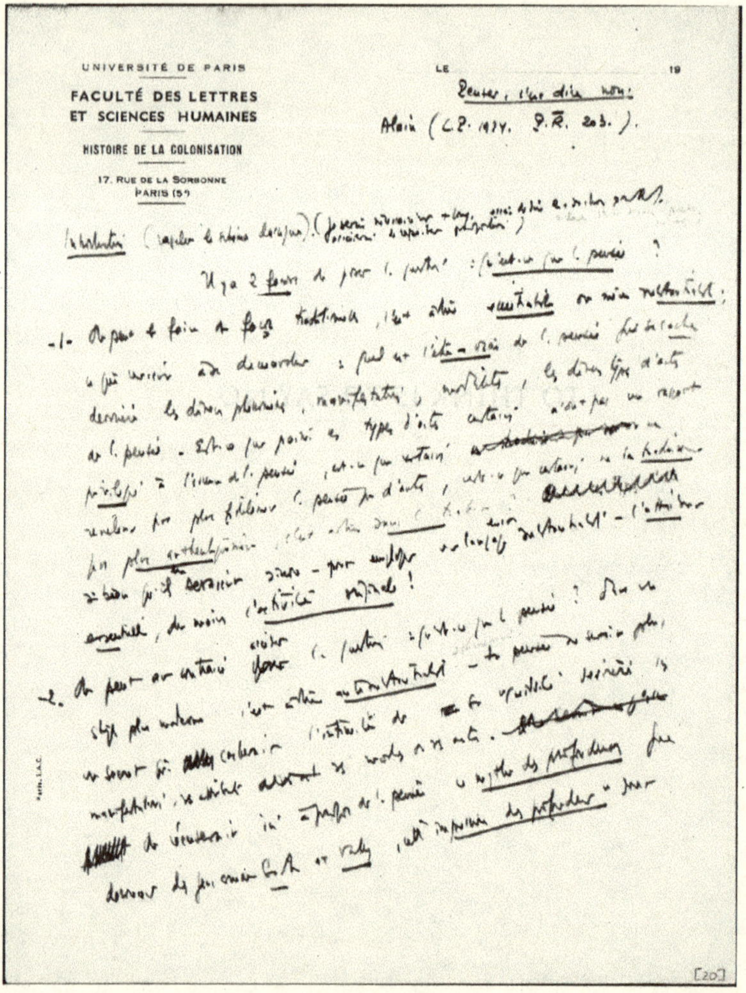
UNIVERSITÉ DE PARIS

FACULTÉ DES LETTRES
ET SCIENCES HUMAINES

HISTOIRE DE LA COLONISATION

17, RUE DE LA SORBONNE
PARIS (5e)

LE 19

[20]

Figure 1. The first page of Derrida's handwritten manuscript.

First Session

"To think is to say no." (1)[1]

ALAIN (L.P. 1924.

P.R. 203)[2]

Introduction (recall the classic schema). (I will necessarily spend more time here and will try to say as many things as possible. [I] will try to respect [the] proportions).[3]

1. The entire text of the manuscript is written on letterhead paper with the following heading: "UNIVERSITÉ DE PARIS/FACULTÉ DES LETTRES ET SCIENCES HUMAINES/HISTOIRE DE LA COLONISATION/17, RUE DE LA SORBONNE PARIS (5e)."

2. Alain, *Philosophie: Textes choisis pour les classes*, ed. Antoinette Drevet (Paris: Presses Universitaires de France, 1957), 1:274. "L. P." is a reference to the journal *Libres Propos*, published by Michel Alexandre between 1921 and 1924, and 1927 and 1935. Alain published many of his *Propos* there. "P. R." refers to a collection of texts by Alain, *Propos sur la religion: Éléments d'éthique politique* (Paris: Éditions Rieder/PUF), 1938. [No complete English translation exists of either of these works. A selection of some fifty *Propos*—including "To think is to say no"—has been translated into English by Michel Petheram and is available on the website of the Association of the Friends of Alain (see https://philosophe-alain.fr/alain-in-english/). We have used Petheram's excellent translations whenever possible but have often had to modify them—like other translations in this work—in order to highlight the key terms that Derrida focuses on in his commentary or to make them consistent with the translation of other texts referenced by Derrida.—Trans.]

3. In the interlinear space there is a penciled addition: "2 starting points (thinking yes no)."

There are 2 *ways* to pose the question: *What is thought?*

1. One can do it in a traditional way, that is to say, in an *essentialist* or even *substantialist* way, which amounts to asking: What is the *true being* of thought that is *hidden* behind the various phenomena, manifestations, modalities, the different kinds of acts of thought? Among these kinds of acts, do some not have a *privileged* relationship to the experience of thought? Do some not reveal thought more faithfully than others? Do some not *translate* thought *more authentically* than others, that is to say, without translating it? In such a way that they would be, if not *its essential attribute*—to use a still substantialist language—at least *its original activity*?

2. One can, on the contrary, approach the question "What is thought?" in a more modern, that is to say, antisubstantialist, style:[4] thought would no longer be a secret that hides the intimacy of its "quiddity" behind its manifestations, its attributes, its words, or its acts. One would here reject, with regard to thought, the *myth of depths* denounced by people like *Sartre* and *Valéry*, this "*impression of depths*," which Bachelard says is a "*superficial impression*." Thought would then be nothing but the *totality of its phenomena*, the *totality of its manifestations*, that is to say, since thought is only what it makes of *itself* [*se* fait], the *totality of its acts*. But if it is the totality of *its* acts, it is because it manifests *itself*; and then, without being anything other than its acts, perhaps it is more *itself* in certain acts than in others, or better still, in order to be the totality of its acts, insofar as they are acts *of* thought, these acts partake of a *fundamental and authentic*

4. In the space between the lines there is an addition: "+ phenomenologically."

activity.[5] You see that the so-called *substantialist*[6] myth is not so easy to exorcise. It imposes itself in the end as soon as one wants to say with any seriousness "*this is that*" or as soon as one asks the question: *What is something?*

Phenomenology. Ontology. The two paths thus converge: One must ask whether certain acts refer to a fundamental and essential activity or attitude of thought.

It might at first seem that, insofar as to think is to try to grasp the *truth*, to say "*what is what*," *this is that*, it might seem that thought is in search of a final *affirmation*, of an *approval* of the true;[7] it might therefore seem that thought is itself, that is, *in agreement with itself*, only when it approves itself, that is, when it says *yes, this is that*, yes, *that is indeed how things are*, which implies, yes, you are right, yes, you are right to think this way.[8] If thought seems to be nothing but *disquiet*, nothing but *discord with itself* and with *the world*, this is only an *appearance*; it is because it is moving toward what it seeks, namely, rest, agreement with itself and reconciliation with the world, that is, yes to itself and to the world. We cannot imagine that something would be its own discord, or its own discordance, its own disagreement with

5. In the manuscript, there is an addition mark indicated by "↔." This symbol is generally used by Derrida as a reminder that he will orally comment on what precedes it.

6. In the manuscript the words "essentialist or" appear crossed out before the word "substantialist."

7. In the manuscript there is an addition mark "↔."

8. An arrow introduces the following: "Is-so it is [*Est-soit*]"—these words are underlined and crossed out. "So it is [*Soit*] [(value) presupposed by ["There is a 'so it is [*soit*]' in every indicative affirmation": These words are crossed out] every indicative utterance that this or that. Normative approval immanent to indicative affirmation (and even to negative utterance)."

itself, its own disorder.[9] For to be something also implies a certain repose of the self, a certain peace between essence and existence, a certain yes of the self to itself and of the self to the world.[10] For how would thought, which alone among beings has the privilege of being able to *say* this *yes*, not be entirely this desire to say yes, this will to affirm itself and the world that would confirm it in its essence?

Thus, in this case, all the "*yeses*," all the acts of thought that have the force and form of affirmation, acquiescence, approval, acceptance, would reveal in a *privileged way* and par excellence the essence of a thought that is always in search of a truth of itself and of the world in which to rest and complete its movement, in search of a certainty or an obviousness [*évidence*] to which it must, as we say, "give itself over [*se rendre*: surrender]."

But "to give oneself over" is "to give over one's arms" (polemics → appearances . . .); is this then not to abdicate? Is it not to dispossess and renounce oneself?—At the moment it says "yes,"[11] does not thought deny [*nie*] itself, does it not renounce itself [*se renier*], does it not say no to itself precisely because this *yes* marks the transition from critical awareness, from the vigilant mistrust of the lookout,[12] the mark of all live or living thought, to the passivity of belief, which always implies some underlying credulity and naivety?—In the *yes*, does not thought, having reached its goal, *abandon itself*, in the sense that to abandon oneself is both to let oneself drift

9. Here in the manuscript there is the beginning of a crossed-out sentence: "Thought, if it is something, is."

10. Here in the manuscript there is the beginning of a crossed-out sentence: "It is therefore in affirmation."

11. In the manuscript there is an addition at the top of the margin that reads: "Flees from [upon] the most constraining evidence."

12. In the manuscript the words "of the lookout" replace the crossed-out words "in belief."

into the lethargic and uncontrolled inertia of sleep, and to take leave of oneself, to separate oneself from one's identity, to become a stranger to oneself? No doubt, the *yes*, approval, affirmation, acceptance are the *end* of thought, the end in the sense of *telos*, in the sense of an ideal pole, a goal; no doubt thought accomplishes itself in the *yes*; but the end in the sense of *telos* is also the end in the sense of termination and limit [*borne*]. When it says "*yes*," thought stops *in the end*; it becomes limited, closed-minded [*bornée*]; it ceases to be, as thought.[13]

Surely thought wants *to give itself over to the truth*; but it is itself only when it gives itself over to the truth in the sense that *giving itself over to* [se rendre à] means *going over toward* [aller vers], that is to say, being on the way toward, overcoming obstacles, denouncing its own cowardice and lethargy, renouncing its inertia, freely refuting mirages and fantasies, refusing to allow any weightiness to make me say *yes* too soon; being on the way toward the truth is thus to affirm my freedom [illegible words][14] power to say no. To be on the way toward the truth is to say no to appearances. But to think is not "to give oneself over" to the truth in the sense that "to give oneself over" is to become subservient, to lose oneself and to hand over one's powers at the moment of saying *yes* to the impostor. In this case thought would indeed be itself, purely itself, at the moment it denies itself [*se nie*]; born [*née*] of this essence of negativity, of this fundamental power of negativity, affirmation would be only a passing mo-

13. In the manuscript here there is a crossed-out beginning of a sentence: "In this case, affirmation, far from," followed by another crossed-out beginning of a sentence introducing the next paragraph: "To think would therefore be to say no."

14. In the manuscript there are one or two illegible words that might be: "that is to say, my."

ment, I would even say an *accident*, in the sense both of the *nonessential* (opposition of accident and essence) and in the sense of *fall*, even of sin against thought. When thought says *yes* to this and that, and falls short of its final destination, it undergoes a fall and becomes itself fallen. The yes would literally be a *lapsus* of thought.

That is why Alain says, "To think is to say no."

1. What, for Alain, justifies such a proposition? Can we take it literally and accept the philosophy that supports it?

2. What does it mean to say no? What is the meaning and origin of "saying no," of negation?

I – (Recall the meaning and necessity of this first development) text or pretext . . .

So what did Alain mean?[15]

In describing the authentic movement of thought as a movement of negation, Alain wanted to remind us that all thought is a *consciousness* [conscience],[16] which,[17] wrongly, might seem [illegible word][18] to be a mere triviality. For there are forms of thought that Alain distrusts and rejects even more violently than simple nonthoughts, i.e., passions and reflexes. These forms of thought betray true thought all the more insofar as they present themselves as pure thought.

15. In the manuscript there is an addition in the form of a series of words that read: "justification / 3 steps—requires cross-examinations → critique."

16. [*Conscience* in French can mean both "consciousness" and "conscience." Derrida, following Alain, will work with both meanings throughout.—Trans.]

17. In the manuscript the following words are crossed out: "seems wrongly like a flat triviality."

18. In the manuscript there is an illegible word that might be: "intuitive."

This is everything, precisely, that can be categorized under the heading of "*science without conscience* [science sans conscience]"; this is the knowledge of those who lose themselves in what they know because, not knowing that they know, they lose all *freedom* with regard to science. This is often what characterizes, in particular, all purely scientific and technical thought, and Alain never tires of denouncing it.

Now, how does "To think is to say no" call us[19] to *consciousness*, that is, to *awakening* and *vigilance*? Listen to Alain: "*To think is to say no. Notice that the sign for yes is that of a man falling asleep; but in waking up he shakes his head and says no.*"[20]

To say *yes* is to incline the head toward sleep and the servitude of thought → everything that is not thought, starting with the body; it is to cease paying attention. Approval is a drowsiness of thought, which, from the moment it has *consented*, is no longer its own *master*, has handed over its powers. It has *subjected* itself; it has found a *master*. That is why Alain deploys this image on the dual plane of the psychology of consciousness, the psychology of waking and sleeping, and political theory. It is indeed by taking up the old Platonic theme of the structural analogy between the soul, the human body, and the city that Alain can also say:

"Once the human head repeats that old movement up and down in order to say yes, the kings promptly return."[21]

This means that when thought says *yes* it alienates itself, alienates its responsibility and will in favor of *another*, that is, inevitably, a nonthought. But any thought, in order to be

19. In the manuscript the word "science" is crossed out.

20. Alain, *Philosophie*, 1:274. In the manuscript the quotation is followed by a crossed-out sentence: "To say no is therefore to awaken or to wake up."

21. *Ibid.*, 278.

a thought, must be responsible for itself, must institute itself alone as judge and master of its own domain. It must make itself a law unto itself. Its sole political regime[22] is *autonomy* or *autarky*.

"The function of thinking cannot be delegated,"[23] says Alain (L. P. 1931. Min[24] 301).

This autonomy or autarky is not, in fact, in Alain's eyes, in contradiction with democracy, provided these notions are correctly understood.

This is why the *yes* is that of a man who is falling asleep, who is resting. Note in passing that this image of Alain is linked to a certain civilization or a certain culture of the body. It would no longer make any sense in a different culture, for example, in the Far East, where the gesture for *no* is our gesture of approval. This is why it is more an image, more an illustration, than a proof. Even in the West, one does not necessarily fall asleep by letting one's head drop down, but sometimes also by letting it go from left to right or right to left, as if to say no. This might encourage us, if we wanted to compete in *speciosity* with Alain, to show that a certain *mechanical no* would lead just as surely to sleep as counting sheep in one's imagination.

—"But in waking up he shakes his head and says no."

The return to consciousness is a *no* (to the body, to dreamlike appearances, to passivity, no "to oneself lying down [*à soi couché*]"). Consciousness is born simultaneously with *re-*

22. In the interlinear space there is the addition: "in the city of men or in the [illegible word that might be 'intellectual'] city."

23. Alain, *Philosophie*, 1:277–78.

24. "Min" here refers to Alain's text *Minerve ou De la sagesse* (Paris: Paul Hartmann, 1939), 301.

fusal. Refusal is thus *congenital*, and therefore *consubstantial* with consciousness. Consciousness is a *negativity*. It *does not come* to say "no" at this or that moment in its history. The "no" does not happen to it; consciousness comes to itself through *the no*. It is the *no* by *nature*, that is, by origin. The no is its birth act, its act of birth or rebirth (if it is a matter of awakening).

(Regarding this essential negativity of consciousness, see Schelling and Sartre, though this is not the place for such an analysis.)

Note that the awakening to which Alain refers is[25] a *startled* [en sursaut] awakening, one that happens without a continuous passage or gentle transition between the body's sleep and the awakening of consciousness. That is because consciousness is a *start* [*sursaut*]; it is a rupture with the body. As we will see, it is a dualism of the Cartesian type, but even more pronounced than that of Descartes, who constantly inspires Alain, and particularly here. Between consciousness and the body, mistrust must be the rule, and cohabitation polemical. Being awake, and especially waking up, is a being startled because it is a *surprising* of the body by thought, which has escaped the body through *effraction* and not through the subservience of the body at rest.

This identification of thought with consciousness in the form of a fundamental *no* allows us to understand a theme dear to Alain, namely, *the intrinsic identity of psychological consciousness and moral conscience*. If there is no psychological consciousness without moral conscience, and if the latter is presupposed by the former, it is because conscious-

25. In the manuscript a few words are crossed out here: "something like."

ness in general is refusal. But what is refusal if not resistance to what is?[26]

To resist what is, is first of all to oppose what ought to be to what is. Refusal is thus, in its essence, moral. Therefore, insofar as all consciousness is this primordial refusal of what is, all consciousness is first of all moral. The most elementary, most rudimentary phenomenon of waking presupposes this will to resist passivity, the magic of appearances, the determinisms of the body, etc. The will to resist is a certain *courage*, a *duty*, and a *moral experience*.[27] Through the *no*, consciousness opens the space that separates being from value. Consciousness does *not therefore become* moral through the understanding of, or through participation in, a constituted morality; consciousness is to be found in obligation and, therefore, in the *no*, which are united and, as it were, in its element. Here is the text from Alain (*Histoire de mes pensées*, 77):

> Professionals distinguish psychological consciousness from moral conscience. To which I first remarked that the word psychological is not part of our Patrimony, and that it is useless to burden oneself with it. But another remark led me further . . . all consciousness is of a moral order, since it always opposes what should be to what is. And even in simple perception, what awakens us from custom is always a sort of scandal [cf., startle . . . trauma. heroism], and an energetic resistance to simple facts. All knowledge . . .

26. In the manuscript the following words are crossed out: "Resistance to what is, to which one."

27. In the manuscript there is an addition: "I inaugurate morality in negation." This addition is followed by another mark indicating an addition: "↔."

begins and continues through *indignant refusals*, in
the very name of the honor of thinking.[28]

That,[29] then, is our first theme: thought = consciousness [*conscience*].

To think is therefore to say no because to think is to be awake, because to think is to be conscious; but to be conscious is to be present to oneself. To negate [*nier*] is a verb that has no real direct object—or rather, its direct object is always a subject: How so?

But then how can "negativity" be the form of presence to oneself? How can the *no* be *consciousness*, that is, consciousness of oneself with oneself [*de soi avec soi*], the dialogue of thought with itself?

It is because, for Alain, the second theme is . . .

The fundamental intransitivity of the no.

To think is to say no. *No to what?* Alain then asks.

I want, first, to emphasize the relatively secondary and derivative character of the question "to what." Too often in your essays you became fixated on the possible objects of negation, and you enumerated everything to which consciousness could say no. But what matters—and first of all to Alain—what is philosophically interesting, is not that thought refuses *this* or *that*, this rather than that, but that it is *refusal itself*[30] and is in itself refusal. What matters is that the "no" is not an order or a rule or a norm, an imperative

28. Alain, *Histoire de mes pensées*, 13th ed. (Paris, Gallimard, "NRF," 1936), 77. Derrida highlights, adds, and omits some words from the original quotation.

29. In the manuscript there is a penciled addition: "transition to be developed."

30. In the interlinear space there is the addition "(refusal ≠ attribute of consciousness. All refusal goes through consciousness)."

given[31] to consciousness with regard to this or that *object*; what matters is that this *no*, before coming up against this or that object, is the very *project* of consciousness. Rejection is, if you will, the very form of the project of consciousness. It is not a sort of external and accidental refutation; it is *constitutive* of consciousness.

This is so true that Alain, after having seemed to answer the question "to what?" adds that the object of negation is only ever an appearance, a detour, or an apparent pretext. In reality, thought never says no to anything; it never says no to anything but itself. It negates nothing in appearance that it does not *in reality* first negate with regard to *itself* as what first believed in the appearance, what first said *yes*. That is why I said earlier that the direct object of negation is always first the subject of negation itself. *To negate is a reflexive verb*,[32] that is, it is first of all to "negate oneself." Here is what Alain says: "No to what? To the *world*, to the *tyrant*, to the *preacher*? That is only the appearance. In each of these cases, thought is saying *no* to itself. It puts an end to happy *acquiescence*. [quietude and inquietude. Happiness of sleep] It separates itself from itself. It struggles against itself. *There is no other struggle in the world*."[33]

Before taking up the three apparent "*noes*" of thought—to the *world*, to the *tyrant*, to the *preacher*—before showing that the dialogue with the *world*, with the *tyrant*, and with the *preacher* is always *preceded and mediated*, as it were, by a dialogue with oneself, Alain insists on the *agonistic* and *polemical* meaning of this dialogue with oneself: "Thought

31. In the manuscript there is a crossed-out word that might be "naturally."

32. In the interlinear space there is the addition "Thought = consciousness but reflected consciousness, reflection, and refusal."

33. Alain, *Philosophie*, 1:274–75.

separates itself from itself. It struggles against itself. *There is no other struggle in the world."* Why is there no other struggle in the world? Because *before* confronting the other and *in order to* confront the other—in all its forms, the other person [*autrui*], the world, the tyrant, the preacher, even the friend—I must confront within myself an inner enemy, an internal defeatist who lulls me to sleep, who counsels flight, who pushes me to give in, to let myself be overcome or won over without examination, without risk. The mind can therefore only ever wage Trojan wars[34] because its enemy is always already on the inside, because the mind can only fight the mind and can let itself be overcome only by itself. This is, in a completely different register,[35] a transposition of the Hegelian theme according to which war is only ever possible between consciousnesses and already presupposes a first interiorization of the other in me. No war in nature. Consciousness and self-contestation.

The *world*, the *tyrant*, the *preacher* are therefore the only three figures through which the mind mediates itself either to enslave itself or to liberate itself, in any case, to constitute for itself an interlocutor in a dialogue with itself.

1. *In what way is the no to the world a no to oneself?*

Well, insofar as every perception, however elementary, natural, or prescientific it may be, is already a *critique of appearance*. To see something, I must abstain from a certain adherence or adhesion to the phenomenon; I must contest the phenomenon, solicit it, question it about what it is in order to be able to know or recognize it.[36]

34. In the manuscript "battles" is crossed out and replaced by "wars."

35. In the manuscript "spirit [*esprit*]" is crossed out and replaced by "register."

36. In the manuscript there is an addition completing the end of the paragraph: "; I must say no to it, but it is my belief to which I say no."

"What do I see when I open my eyes? What would I see if I had to believe everything? In truth, a hodgepodge of forms and colors, like an incomprehensible tapestry."[37] To believe everything, and thus to say *yes* to everything, is to choose to see nothing. At bottom, the *epoché*, this suspension of judgment on which the skeptics were the first to insist, together with this *skepsis*, which means *visual* attention before meaning *doubt*, this *epoché* and this *skepsis*, before being philosophical revolutions, are the indispensable conditions of all perception. To see something is a whole process, requiring any number of implicit selections, critiques, questions.[38] And it is only by doing violence to myself, by doing violence to the blissful inertia of my intuition—which, Kant already said, was *blind* without the understanding—that I am truly able to perceive the world.[39] Alain:

> For[40] it is by questioning myself about each thing that I see it. A lookout shading his eyes with his hand is a man who says no [who scrutinizes].[41] In the war, the lookouts stationed in observatories for days on end learned to see, always by saying no. And astronomers through the centuries have always pushed the moon, the sun, and the stars further away from us by saying no. Notice that when the whole of existence first presented itself to us, everything was true; this pres-

37. Alain, *Philosophie*, 1:275.

38. In the manuscript the following beginning of a sentence is crossed out: "And these questions, it is first to myself that I pose them, to myself who would spontaneously confuse them."

39. In the interlinear space there is an addition of three words that are both underlined and crossed out: "πίστις and cave."

40. In the original quotation Alain writes: "But it is by questioning myself . . ."

41. In the manuscript there is a mark indicating an addition: "↔."

> ence of the world never deceives. The sun appears no larger than the moon; it must therefore not appear otherwise, based on its distance and size. And the sun rises in the east for the astronomer as well; that's where it should appear in accordance with the movement of the earth on which we are being carried. But it is also *our* business to put everything back in its place and at its distance. It is therefore indeed to *myself* that I say *no*.[42]

To perceive, therefore, one must be on the *lookout* (images distorted by water). Spontaneous consciousness[43] is *phenomenal* and *Don Quixotesque*: it *believes* that things are as they first appear to it. And if it does not question itself, if it does not *detach* itself from this first adherence, if it does not upset [*déçoit*] this first adherence to the world, it will perceive only its own fantasies, that is to say, *nothing*.[44] Imagination will prevail over understanding. To want to say no to oneself is to acknowledge the fact that all perception is fundamentally a possibility of deception [*déception*: or disappointment], just as all questioning is therefore fundamentally a possibility of *negation*. That is why, at least for Alain, one is always responsible for one's own illusions or errors. One is not responsible for having seen giants. One is responsible for having yielded to this appearance, for having *opined*, for having *judged*, by saying: *yes*, those are giants. Common sense points out this responsibility, this culpability in error, when it says that one is *deluding oneself* [se trompe].

42. Alain, *Philosophie*, 1:275. Derrida's emphasis and addition of the words in brackets.

43. In the interlinear space there are two added words: "affirmation, credulous."

44. [The French *décevoir* can mean either "to deceive" or "to disappoint." Derrida will work with both meanings in what follows.—Trans.]

It is oneself that one is deluding, through a certain act of will, by assenting [*opinant*] prematurely to one's impression and belief. Error is first of all a fault, a sin against thought, and presupposes a malevolence of the will. The one who makes an error is never innocent. He could have said no.

This analysis is, of course, in line with a voluntarism and a philosophy of judgment and, even, on this specific point, a Cartesian philosophy of judgment, for Descartes indeed places a great deal of emphasis on the role of the will in judgment. To judge is to opine by an act of will, to say yes to a perception of our understanding. Understanding perceives an idea but does not itself have the power to judge. It is the will that, by an act, converts perception into judgment and allows us to affirm "*this is that*," the idea is true. Consequently, for Descartes too it is already the will that is responsible for error, that is to say, for false opinion; being infinite, it always exceeds the understanding, which is finite; it can therefore rush on ahead [*se précipiter*] and assent to [*opiner*] what understanding does not see well.[45]

So that's the *no to the world*, which is first of all a *no to oneself*. It is easy to extrapolate from this what the other noes to oneself might be, in the form of the *no to the tyrant* and the *no to the preacher*.

2. *The tyrant*. "What makes the tyrant my master," says Alain in the same text, "is the fact that I respect rather than examine."[46]

For tyranny and, consequently, servitude to be possible, I must have said *yes* and ceased to criticize. But here again, it is first a matter of a *yes to oneself*, "*to oneself lying down*,"

45. In the manuscript there is a mark at the end of the paragraph indicating an addition: "↔."

46. Alain, *Philosophie*, 1:275.

for if I persist in refusing, the tyranny will remain external; it will be servitude of the body, that is, freedom of the mind. It is I who, thanks to the freedom of my mind, will always determine the tyrant's power. The tyrant needs my *yes* to make me his slave. Here again, as in Hegel, the master, who needs the assent and recognition of the slave, becomes at a certain moment the slave of the slave, just as the slave becomes the master of the master. A Stoic and Cartesian theme . . .

This theory of tyranny is again valid here, as in Plato, both as a theory of political tyranny and as a theory of the psychological tyranny of the soul subjected to passion.

Cartesian [illegible word] development.

3. Finally, the *no to oneself* as *no to the preacher*.

The preacher is not a master of error; he is a master of *belief*. *Dogma*, by essence and etymology, is what one *believes*, the object of a *doxa*. As for doxa, it is both belief and *opinion*, in the sense that to opine is to say yes. Dogma is what one says yes to without any discussion because it is the authority, and so without thinking, since thinking [*penser*] is examining, contesting authority, *weighing* [peser], as Alain also says, referring to the origin of the word.

Now the preacher is someone who appeals only to arguments of authority. He is someone who wants to teach me religion through belief in dogma, *belief* being always vigorously opposed by Alain to *faith*. Belief stops at the phenomenon, at what Alain calls the *sign*: It stops at the symbol and the letter, whereas faith seeks to understand the symbolism beyond the symbol, the spirit beyond the letter. Thus, saying no to the preacher is saying no to the sign in order to understand the meaning.[47] Now, the sign is a sign only through

47. In the manuscript there is the beginning of a sentence that is crossed out: "And to say no to the sign is to say no to oneself who *believes* in belief."

my belief. It is therefore to my belief, to me as a believer, that I must say no.

> All religion is true, in the same way that the first appearance of the world is true. But that does not take me very far. I must say no to the signs. There is no other way to understand them. Always rubbing one's eyes and scrutinizing the sign is what it means to be on the watch and to think. Otherwise one is sleeping. However determined one may be to believe everything, it is still true that Jesus is something other than that child in the manger. One must pierce the appearance. The Pope himself does so in each of his prayers. Would it be prayer otherwise? No, just the sleep of an *old man*. [[48]formation of signs?] Behind the sign, there is theology. But if theology is only a sign, then what is it? And what is behind theology? One must understand, which is always to say no. No, you are not what you seem to be. As the astronomer says to the sun; as any man says to the image distorted by water. And what is scruple [scruples—little worries—weights—obstacles], if not saying no to what one believes? The examination of conscience [religious sense] is saying no to oneself lying down. What I believe is never enough, and incredulity is a strict faith. "Take up thy bed, and walk."[49]

So,[50] a critique of belief in general, which will be examined directly in the third major part of this development

48. In the manuscript there is a mark indicating an addition: "↔."

49. Alain, *Philosophie*, 1:275–76. Derrida underscores and adds the words in brackets. [The closing quotation is from John 5:8—Trans.]

50. In the margin there is an addition preceded by an arrow pointing to the beginning of the paragraph: "—no to the preacher."

dedicated to Alain (recall the first two: thinking = consciousness. Intransitivity of negation or negation and reflection).

We will see:
1. What the general philosophical presuppositions of Alain's formulation are.
2. How we will find within Alain's thought elements for going beyond this formulation (to think: to say no).
3. How, on the basis of this going beyond, the essay can → general significance.[51]

51. In the manuscript there is a mark indicating an addition: "↔."

Second Session

"To think is to say no." (2)

After having indicated the different paths from which one might approach this question, we defined its terms.[1] We saw how an inquiry into the negativity of thought ought to be understood. This negativity could be *either* a constitutive essence *or* an accidental modalization of thought.

Then, having posed the question, we began in a first development to examine Alain's response, attempting to understand and justify it in and of itself and on its own terms. This was to be done in *three stages*, which would guide us toward the core and general presuppositions of Alain's thought insofar as they frame the phrase in question.

The first stage involved the negativity of thought in the essential form of vigilant *waking consciousness*. Refusal appeared to us as *congenital* and *consubstantial* to thought, which, insofar as it is awake, is a will to *autarky* and *autonomy* and is first of all "*moral*" inasmuch as it is *psychological*, since, through this refusal of being and doing, it establishes the order[2] of the ought-to-be and of value.

1. In the manuscript, a few crossed-out words appear at the beginning of the paragraph: "The last time, after posing the problem of knowing."

2. [While the French edition has *ombre* (shadow) here, the manuscript seems to say *ordre* (order). — Trans.]

From there, we moved to a *second stage*, where the question of *the origin of negation* arose, the question of "*to what*" no is being said. This led to a discussion in Alain of the theme of what I called *the fundamental intransitivity of a negation* that never has a direct object except in appearance because it is, in reality, first and foremost a *no of thought to itself*, a reflexive negativity. The no to the *world*, to the *tyrant*, to the *preacher*, which we explained in succession, each referred to a no to oneself, a no to *oneself lying down*, and, on a deeper level, to a *voluntarist* and *Cartesian* philosophy of *judgment*, *error*, and *fault*. The no to the *preacher*, as we saw, was a no to the *believing* self,[3] that is, to the *dogmatic* self, *the philosophical self*. And from there it led to what I believe to be the ultimate source of Alain's phrase, namely, a "critique of belief," which we will now examine in the third and final stage of this first development.

* * *

3. This *radical critique of belief*, which is characteristic of a voluntarist philosophy of freedom and judgment, will allow us better to determine and at the same time to limit the scope of Alain's formulation. If it is first of all and essentially a critique of belief, it is not really to itself that thought says no but to this idol[4] or to this degradation of authentic thought that *believing* thought, that *credulous* thought, is. For, as Alain says elsewhere, "the incredulous mind is the

3. In the interlinear space there is an addition of four words that are difficult to decipher but might be: "in all its forms."

4. In the manuscript the following words are crossed out: "of authentic thought."

mind *tout court*" (L. P. 1934).[5] Belief is indeed a certain attitude [illegible word][6]; it is this naive and banal *yes* that must be silenced; and it must be silenced because it is prior to [*en deçà*] judgment. It is passive and gives itself over, tied and bound, to the first appearance or the first authority. It is the hold over us that we ourselves hand over to the *dogmatist* and the *preacher* by renouncing a judgment that is in essence a nonjudgment. That is why the preacher's discourse, that is, *preaching* [*prédication*], is always the language of prejudice, even if this prejudice happens to be true. The preacher always addresses *nature* and the *body*, which in themselves do not know how to refuse. So there is a dualism of mind and nature, a Cartesian dualism, that is of a piece with a mechanism of nature that supports this critique of belief. Regarding the phrase "to think," Alain writes: "It is to weigh what comes to mind, to suspend one's judgment, to control oneself, and not to be complacent. . . . *It is therefore a refusal of natural thought*, and, at its deepest level, *a refusal of nature*, which indeed is not the judge of thoughts."[7]

What seems particularly interesting to me in this refusal of *dogma* as a refusal of nature is that, through it, *thought* is not defined in its *authenticity* on the basis of anything other than itself, and particularly not on the basis of *truth*, that is, in the classical sense, on the basis of adequation to the ob-

5. Alain, *Philosophie: Textes choisis pour les classes*, ed. Antoinette Drevet (Paris: Presses Universitaires de France, 1957), 1:250.

6. In the manuscript there is an illegible word that might be "ours."

7. Alain, *Philosophie*, 1:258. Derrida underscores and truncates the following quotation: "It is to weigh what comes to mind, to suspend one's judgment, to control oneself, and not to be complacent. To think is to go from one idea to everything that is opposed to it, in order to align all thoughts with that one thought. *It is therefore a refusal of natural thought*, and, at its deepest level, *a refusal of nature*, which indeed is not the judge of thoughts. To think is therefore to judge that not everything within us is as it appears; it is a long process and a prior peace."

ject. This means, quite simply, the following: Even if what I *believe* is *true*, my thought is in error. It errs not because it falls short [*manque*] of the object but because it falls short of itself. Or else, if you like, *the true can never be the object of a belief*. To believe is to be not free to judge, and the true, to be true, presupposes that one goes to it freely. And it is in this free movement that thought is itself. And the true is nothing without this freedom of judgment. It is freedom that constitutes truth as such. That is why teaching is such a difficult thing. It would be easy—there would be nothing to it—if its task were simply to transmit the truth. It must also teach thought, which is something other than a technique of truth; and as soon as truth is tied to a technique, well, one is already the victim of those two falsifications of thought, apparently distant from one another and even contradictory, but whose affinity no doubt runs deep: sophistry and dogmatism.

L. P. 1922. Min. 43.
Comment in detail:

> A continuous and very skillfully directed pressure is exerted against the mind. There is a way of teaching, whether it be science, languages, or history, that stubbornly goes against the mind. The old apprenticeship, which is nothing but slavery, is returning everywhere under the guise of *technical knowledge*. [cf. science without conscience] In short, I say that the mind has done nothing yet; but that is because it is not yet awake. We venerate a heap of large stones, and true believers bring every day yet another stone. Such is the tomb of Descartes.[8]
>
> We should dare; we do not dare. But does one

8. In the manuscript there is a mark here indicating an addition: "↔."

really know? The doctrine of free judgment is deeply buried. I see hardly anyone but believers. *They do have this scruple, to believe only what is true. But what one believes is never true.*[9]

In other words, the *yes*, even if it is uttered at the end of the most critical examination, even if it is absolutely well-founded, converts *consciousness* into *belief* and *truth* into *dogma*. Suppose that, "inspired" by a radical mistrust, I refuse to accept evidence indefinitely on the pretext that it might be only an appearance, up until the moment when I possess the absolute *proof* of the truth of the evidence: then, I say *yes*, yes to the *truth*; but the very moment I consent, however necessary and well-founded my consent may be, I have begun to *believe* and ceased to *think* until the moment when I again shake my belief. At bottom it is the idea of proof as a technical instrument of truth that Alain refuses here; it is proof or the system as a reassuring haven and shelter of truth that must be constantly destroyed.[10] Truth is never in an object; truth is not a treasure; it is not a secret that one puts in reserve; it is something to be endlessly begun anew. This critique of belief leads us to *three conclusions* that will help us both to better understand Alain and to be wary, for our own part, of his formulation. In other words, to be faithful to Alain one must perhaps know how to refuse a dogmatism of negation.

First conclusion: the refusal of proof as a putting in abeyance [*mise en sommeil*] of truth leads Alain to an *ultraradi-*

9. Alain, *Philosophie*, 1:273; "Le tombeau de Descartes," in *Minerve ou De la sagesse (Paris: Paul Hartmann, 1939)*, 43. Derrida's emphasis. In the manuscript there is a mark here indicating an addition: "↔."

10. In the margin of the manuscript there is an addition: "Proof tires out the truth."

calism[11] of doubt that his master Descartes might not have accepted. To be sure, Alain's doubt is still a *methodical* doubt and not a *skeptical or nihilistic* doubt, but it is a methodical doubt that has no end. Whereas "method," that is, according to its etymology, the "path one takes" to get to the truth, has an end, which is the truth.[12] And in Descartes first of all.

Alain, as we will see in the text, is a *Descartes without God* or rather *a Descartes whose God is not Cartesian*. Alain is a Descartes who, wishing to be more faithful to Cartesianism than Descartes himself, constantly wants to repeat the gestures that Descartes deemed sufficient to perform once and for all. Seen from the outside and expressed in the language of a psychologist, this resembles a repetition compulsion. Starting from the traumatic scene that is the first experience of radical doubt, one can only from then on repeat the initial scenario.[13] In reality and more deeply, it is the realization that doubt has value in itself, that it is the salvation[14] of thought more than its instrument.

> Doubt is the salt of the mind [cf. Lagneau, Alain's teacher]; without the touch of doubt, all knowledge soon rots. I mean even the best-founded and most reasonable knowledge. Doubting when one realizes one was wrong or deceived is not difficult; I would even say that it doesn't get us anywhere[15]; this *forced*

11. In the manuscript Derrida replaces "hyperradicalism" by "ultraradicalism."

12. In the manuscript there is a mark indicating an addition: "↔."

13. In the manuscript there is this addition in the interlinear space: "(Leibniz ≠)."

14. In the manuscript "the salvation" replaces "the essence," the latter being crossed out.

15. In the margin of the manuscript there is a vertical line alongside the quotation and an addition: "Comment on other philosophers."

> *doubt* is like a violence done to us; it is a sad doubt; it is a doubt of weakness; it is regret for having believed, for having one's trust betrayed. The truth is that one should never believe and should always examine. Incredulity has not yet shown its full measure.[16]

For Alain, what is proper to incredulity is that when it shows its measure it no longer has any measure.[17] It is measureless, *immeasurable*, *immoderate*. And it is by the measure of this immeasurability that truth is measured. There is truth only by the measure of incredulity. This is what is expressed, in substance, by this text, where fidelity to the Cartesian spirit seems to me to be an infidelity to the spirit of Descartes.

> L. P. 1924. P. R. 23.[18]
>
> There is something dead in all Theology, something dead also in all Geometry. These are ideas under lock and key; no one goes to see them anymore, and they are accounted for by registers and summaries, as bookkeepers do [cf. Husserl]. Now, these provisions for the mind spoil even faster than provisions for the mouth. And what is an idea that one does not think about? Bossuet proves God through eternal truths. "A truth cannot cease to be a truth. Descartes dies,

16. Alain, *Philosophie*, 1:277.

17. In the interlinear space between the quotation and the following paragraph, the following was added and then crossed out: "Illustration: Leibniz's thought on Descartes: if one starts doubting, one can never lift this doubt. Therefore, no doubt ≠ Alain."

18. "P. R. 23" refers to *Propos sur la religion* and to December 20, 1923, the date on which this *Propos* by Alain was written.

> Bossuet dies, but the truth does not die. But since a truth is nothing without some thinking being, there therefore exists an eternal Thinking Being." Here is the thought of a disciple and a cupboard of ideas.[19] Descartes is much harder to follow because he breaks the cupboard of ideas and the ideas themselves, going so far as to say that there are no eternal truths at all and that God's will decides upon them at every moment, even for the triangle and the circle. Let those who can, understand. In any case, there is here a scandal and an opportunity to doubt the undoubtable; so it is that Descartes' theology is animated by incredulity.[20]

Of course, Descartes never said there were no eternal truths. On the contrary, and Alain certainly knows this better than anyone. Descartes simply said that God was the creator of eternal truths and that this creation was a continuous creation. Which means, of course, that God could very well make the truth of triangles be called into question. That is within His power. But, Descartes immediately specifies, He cannot wish to use this power because it is in His essence that the ways He chooses are simple and immutable.[21] Of course, continuous creation is conservation only in the eyes of humans, but this continuous creation, to be in accordance with God's essence, must be a recommencement without reversal; in the end, it is the very definition of the truthful God

19. In the manuscript Derrida adds within the quotation: "↔ . . (cf. Delegation). . ."

20. Alain, *Philosophie*, 1:276.

21. In the manuscript there is a mark indicating an addition: "↔." Derrida is referring here to the "Fifth Meditation" of Descartes' *Meditations on First Philosophy*.

that Descartes, as we have seen,[22] so much needs.[23] That is what Alain does not want to hear from Descartes: the apparatus of proofs, the guarantees of divine truthfulness, trust in a truth for which I do not have evidence at the moment, in a word, absolute certainty.[24]

Alain needs a God in the image of his doubter, of one who is incredulous, a God who is no longer a guarantor because He doubts and can start over endlessly. A God who is not reassuring, on whom one cannot rely. In the end Alain would have preferred that we stick with the hypothesis of the deceiving God and even of the Evil Genius in order to save thought and the initiation of thought—thought being initiated only in the no. He must therefore introduce a certain negativity into God so that man can never rest in the positivity of some absolute proof.[25] That is why Alain interprets and deliberately distorts the granting of the creation of eternal truths in a "finitist"[26] sense. It might be said that thought, in its very exercise, is, in a sense, atheistic.[27]

This is why Alain's geometer bears very little resemblance to the Cartesian geometer, that of Descartes and

22. Derrida is likely referring here to a course he gave in 1960–1961 titled "Essence Existence," in which he discusses Descartes's "Fifth Meditation" and the proof of the existence of God. It is also worth mentioning here that, in the spring of 1963, Derrida devoted two courses to Husserl, the first on the notion of God, titled "Phenomenology. Theology. Teleology. Husserl's God," and the second on the fifth of Husserl's *Cartesian Meditations*. See note 3 in the preface.

23. In the manuscript, the following sentence is crossed out: "Alain needs a God who doubts and even one who can deceive."

24. See MS at Princeton: [MSC001_B04_F16_0073].

25. In the interlinear space the following was added: "(inferior, < illegible word >) already to creation."

26. In the manuscript there is a mark indicating an addition: "↔."

27. In the manuscript several words are crossed out: "True geometer. (≠ Descartes ≠ Malebranche). Geometer (Alain—Diderot)."

that of Malebranche.[28] Alain (from the text read earlier): "Descartes' theology is animated by incredulity. Out with the idols. So goes the true Geometer, always doubting and undoing, so that ideas are born and reborn. For I hold that if one wants to know what a straight line is, one must think about it always, I mean to want it and always maintain it, *which is to doubt and to believe together.*"[29]

geo. *creator. responsible. reactivate.*[30]

Second conclusion: a more difficult point. This general critique of belief, as we have just understood it, leads us to a *dualism* that no longer has the same meaning as that between mind and nature, consciousness and body, freedom and mechanism, the kind of dualism to which the analysis of the negativity of thought referred, as you will recall. We now face a necessary and immanent dialectic of thought around this schema. Belief is nothing other than thought, an effect of the body, of nature, etc. It is not a kind of psychological function nor even an autonomous psychological attitude that would come into play when thought falls asleep. It is not an inevitability external to thought. It is not simply a nonfreedom that accidentally limits the freedom of the mind. It is, on the contrary, a necessary moment of the mind in its movement toward the true. "The geometer must believe and doubt at the same time," said Alain.[31] When faced with the true, I cannot do otherwise than to believe and say yes. Once I have said *yes* to the *true*, I must imme-

28. In the manuscript there is a mark at the bottom of the page indicating an addition, "↔," as well as the addition of the word "hallucination."

29. Alain, *Philosophie*, 1:276. Derrida's emphasis.

30. In the manuscript these four words are listed one after another. The last three are underlined. The first is likely an abbreviation for "geometer."

31. Derrida is here likely paraphrasing.

diately *awaken* my belief so that the true does not become an inert, dead thing, a sign or a system. But this awakening itself has no meaning without the *yes.*[32] Belief and doubt are but two dialectically linked moments—the one as necessary as the other—of thought. The putting into abeyance [*mise en sommeil*] of doubt is not a mere passion of the soul, and thus an action of the body as in the Cartesian dualism. It is the very breath of thought, a rhythmic phase of thought, a *necessary period* of thought.[33]

If the *yes* of belief in the true is as *vital* for thought, for consciousness, and for truth as the *no*, well then, one might already begin to wonder whether thinking is saying *no* rather than *yes*, or what a no would be that is not nourished by a yes. In other words, by moving within Alain's thought from the dualism of mind/nature to a deeper dualism that underlies it and is immanent to thought itself, at the very moment when one truly understands what no as thought's no to itself means, one becomes aware that the no to itself is coessential with a yes-to-itself—a yes to itself that follows the no as much as it precedes it and without which the no would be a sterile gesture, a tic rather than a thought. Dialectic of temporality ≠ Descartes ≠ instant.

This leads us to the *third and final conclusion*, which will reveal to us the *yes of belief* and therefore *the no to belief*, the yes of faith and fidelity that motivates all negative and dubitative movement.

32. In the manuscript there is a mark indicating an addition, "↔," along with the words "necessary failing."

33. In the manuscript there is a mark after the paragraph indicating an addition, "↔," along with the words: "The blinking of the eyes [illegible word, which might be "non-being"] → madness ≠ truth."

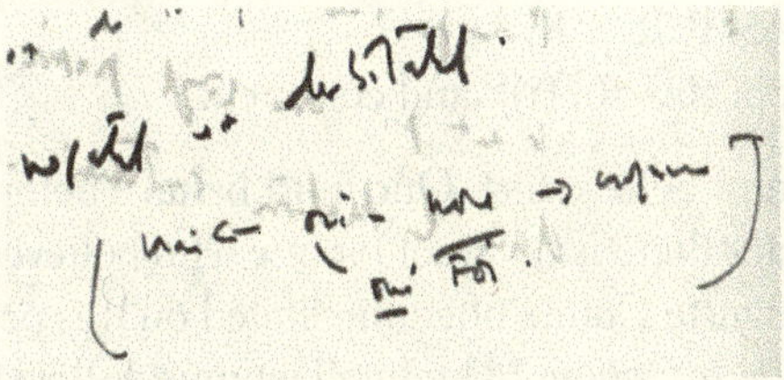

Figure 2. Detail from Derrida's handwritten manuscript.

(true [*vrai*] ←yes [*oui*] – no [*non*]→belief [*croyance*])
yes [*oui*]/ Faith [*Foi*]

Here[34] we reach a deeper level of *radicality*, and it should come as no surprise that we now encounter—still in Alain's work—certain . . . reflections [*propos*] that seem to contradict what we have understood about them up until now. Indeed, to say no, to doubt, to refuse, one must *will* to do so, one must *decide* to do so. There must be a *fiat* or a "so be it" [*soit*] that is a *yes* to the *will to say no*. I say no to this belief, to this content of belief, but I say *yes to the value* and to the will to *truth* in the name of which I say no. And this belief in value precedes the naive belief of credulity, and thus the no to naive belief. The axiological *yes* is fundamental. Willing = affirmation. Voluntarism cannot be a philosophy of negation. This is why Alain writes, in a text that seems to contest "to think is to say no," these words, which actually establish and grant the gravity and seriousness of "to think is to say no."

34. In the manuscript, at the top of the page, there is a crossed-out sentence: "The yes that we have just discovered to be dialectically related to the no was in some way symmetrical to the no."

L. P. 1921 P. R. p. 87
Read pp. 260–261 (1)[35] and comment.

One must believe first. One must believe before any proof, for there is no proof for one who believes nothing. Auguste Comte often meditated on this passage from the *Imitation*: "The intellect must follow faith, not precede it; still less must it break it." If I do not believe that it depends on me to think well or poorly, I let my thoughts drift aimlessly; my opinions wander within me like passersby on a bridge. This is not how Ideas are formed; one must want, choose, and maintain. What interest can I find in a proof, if I do not firmly believe that it will still be good tomorrow? What interest, if I do not firmly believe that the proof that is good for me is good for everyone? But this I cannot prove; every proof presupposes it. In what tone would Socrates explain geometry to the slave boy if he were not sure of finding in this human form the same Reason he had saved within himself?[36]

Thus two beliefs: Faith and credulity. It is faith that says no to credulity.
Faith and madness (don't forget *Zweifelsucht* = madness of doubt).
Pure credulity = madness ([1] < illegible word >[37] = pure negativity)

35. This number (1) appears in the margin of Derrida's copy of Alain's *Philosophie*.

36. Alain, *Philosophie*, 1:260–261.

37. In the manuscript there is an illegible word that might be "nonbeing."

The "madman is a man who believes himself."[38]

The only safeguard = faith.[39] Read p. 260 "There is believing and then there is believing . . ."[40]

Faith = reason.

Negativity = thought.

To say no, thought must first say yes to itself, be sure of itself.

One must be sure *first* = *fidelity*. To precede the event in order to understand it.

"I have often said that fidelity is the light of the mind; this is because I know it. As soon as one changes one's ideas according to the event, intelligence is nothing but a harlot."[41]

Thus, not only has Alain's commentary led us to the opposite of a "to think is to say no," but it has reopened the debate to the fullest possible extent. We have seen that, for Alain, the *yes* and the *no* maintain complex relations of solidarity that change meaning depending on the level of rational-

38. Alain, *Philosophie*, 1:259.

39. In the manuscript Derrida has drawn a box around these words.

40. Alain, *Philosophie*, 1:260. "There is believing and then there is believing, and this difference appears in the words belief (*croyance*) and faith (*foi*). The difference even goes so far as to be an opposition; for according to common language, and in the ordinary course of life, when one says that a man is credulous, one is saying that he lets himself think just about anything, that he submits to appearances, that he succumbs to opinion, that he has no backbone. But when one says that a man of action has faith, one means precisely the opposite. This meaning, so human, so clear to everyone, is distorted by those who want to be believed. For they praise faith, they say that faith saves, and at the same time they reduce faith to the level of the most foolish belief. This cloud is not likely to be dissipated anytime soon. Let us enter into it; it is already nothing more than fog. One can make out a few outlines; it is better than nothing."

41. Alain, *Philosophie*, 1:267.

ity at issue. The question thus remains open. But the way we were led to overturn the initial form of Alain's thought simply through our commentary on it leads us, in the second part that follows, to focus our inquiry on the meaning of this "yes" that is no longer that of credulous naivete but of faith. What is this *yes* that not only is not contradicted but is expressed under the guise of a *no*? What does "to think is to say yes" mean in this new and deeper sense? And what legitimizes this new assertion?

Second (major part).[42] Let us first note, very simply, that contrary to what Alain seemed to think, no *yes* could be entirely *naive* and *credulous*. The *yes* is something that *is said*. Alain says: To think is *to say* no. And *saying*, speech in general, implies an initial break with blissful innocence and sheer unconsciousness, with naive passivity; in a word, a break with a preobjective participation in being, a break with *belief*. Even if it is a *yes* of credulity, this credulity is not *natural*; it is credulity that presupposes a certain fundamental choice and, therefore, this detachment and, therefore, this initial negativity that founds . . . if only the *recitative* attitude of the speaking subject (Goldstein[43] [illegible word] symbolic attitude [illegible word])[44]. . . . Easy enough.

Deep sleep, or even Alain's madman, the one who, he says, is complete belief or credulity in himself, assuming this could exist in a pure state, would be just as incapable of the *yes* as the *no*. Dreamless sleep, the dream itself, pure mad-

42. In the manuscript, at the top of the page, there is an addition: "To think *is to say* yes."

43. Derrida is likely referring to the German psychiatrist and neurologist Kurt Goldstein (1878–1965), whose work influenced philosophers such as Maurice Merleau-Ponty and Georges Canguilhem.

44. In the manuscript there is an illegible word that might be "Deleuze."

ness are domains where language is no longer governed by the categories of negation or affirmation. A concrete analysis is possible here (child—animal—etc.). With the *yes* and the *no*, we have always already separated ourselves from nature.

This point established, we must now distinguish between the *yes* of faith (according to Alain) and the *yes* or *no* of thought in action, of thought at work, and see how the yes of faith is *presupposed* by this thought in action. (Faith = emptied of all specific religious meaning.) With Alain, we have learned *two certainties*:

1. The no *opens* the space of axiology.[45]
2. The *yes* of faith founds this axiological space.

So what does this affirmative founding mean?

This is a question we will examine *successively* and *progressively* under its two main aspects. Axiology, or the theory of norms, or the theory of value, has a *speculative* sense (the true is a *norm*). It also has a *practical* sense (the Good is also a norm).

1. In its *speculative sense*, it seems to resist two forms of negation, which are also two forms of *doubt*. There is no need to insist at length.

—*Skeptical doubt*:[46]

First, it must not be forgotten that the reason why skeptical doubt is so *formidable* [*redoutable*] is that it is not a *simple* refusal of all affirmation; it puts into question both

45. In the manuscript there is a mark indicating an addition, "↔," followed by the words "inaugurates the reign of value."

46. From here to the end of the session, Derrida draws extensively from Victor Brochard's *Les sceptiques grecs* (Paris: J. Vrin, 1959), 54–55. Brochard, a French philosopher (1848–1907), bases his summary largely on the work of the Greek biographer Diogenes Laertius.

affirmation and negation. It is discourse itself as the common ground of the yes and the no whose possibility is struck by the famous *epoché*[47] (suspension of judgment). All things, in themselves, are equally indifferent and indiscernible, and neither our sensations nor our judgments teach us either the true or the false, says Pyrrho. Consequently, we must trust neither the senses nor reason, but remain without *opinion*, leaning neither one way nor the other, in total impassibility. Whatever the matter at hand, one has no more right to affirm it than to deny it, or one must affirm it and deny it at the same time, or one must neither affirm it nor deny it. Equal reasons can always be given for and against each opinion (*antilogia—isostheneia*). Whence such expressions as: "I define nothing" (*ouden horizo*). "Nothing is intelligible." "Neither *yes* nor *no*." But these expressions are still *too affirmative* for Pyrrho; one must understand that, in saying that he affirms nothing, the skeptic is not even affirming this. The words "*no more* this than that" have neither an *affirmative* sense marking equality, as when one says: the pirate *is no more* wicked than the liar, nor a *comparative* sense, as when one says: "honey *is no more sweet* than grapes," but a *negative* sense, as when one says: "There is no more Scylla than there is chimera." This negativity seemed still too *affirmative* to those who replaced the expression *ouden mallon* (neither yes nor no: nothing more) with the *interrogative* expression (*ti mallon*). In all these expressions, affirmation—whether in its affirmative or negative form—was only apparent; it destroys itself, say the skeptics, "like the fire that vanishes with the wood it consumed," "like a purgative that disappears without a trace after cleansing the stomach."

47. Derrida writes "έποχὲ" [*sic*] in the manuscript. In the interlinear space above this word appears the word "skepsis."

Third Session

"To think is to say no." (3)

A few points of reference, as usual.

After our introduction, we had reached the third stage of the first part devoted to a commentary on Alain's thought. This third stage was supposed to show us that the identification of thought with a *vigilant consciousness* (first stage) and the *fundamental intransitivity of negation* (second stage) implied (third < stage >) a *radical critique of belief*, which is the ultimate ground of Alain's phrase.

This *critique of belief* was also a critique of technical knowledge, of the technique of truth, that is, of *proof* in general—a proof that, as Braque says in a phrase that Alain could have endorsed, "*tires out the truth*."[1] If truth can never be the object of a proof upon which it rests, it is because it can never be the object of a belief. This is a theme we commented on at length, and it led us to *three conclusions*:

1. The *ultraradicalism of a doubt* that, in Alain, aimed to be more Cartesian than Descartes's own doubt and that stripped Cartesianism of its entire apparatus of certainty, in particular of a truthful God who guarantees the eter-

1. Georges Braque, *Le jour et la nuit: Cahiers de Georges Braque, 1917–1952* (Paris: Gallimard, 1952), 34. "Proofs tire out the truth."

nal truths He has created. Alain takes away everything that might be reassuring about Him in Descartes.

2. A *dualism of belief and living thought,* a living and dubitative thought that does not admit the dualisms of mind-nature, consciousness-body, freedom-mechanism from which we started, and which paradoxically led to grounding the necessity of dogmatic failure within living thought and linking it dialectically to the necessity of critical awakening. This critical awakening thereby lost its revelatory privilege.

3. Finally, this required us to go down to a level where *the critique of belief* is inseparable from a *praising of faith,* whose meaning we began to clarify. It was a matter there of an axiological *yes,* a yes to the norm or to the value of truth, to the will to truth.

Having thus fully opened the debate, we were led, in a *second major part,* to question the meaning and value of this axiological yes of faith. That is, by showing that "saying *yes* or *no*" could never be "natural," even in credulity, since this implied a break with a primitive participation in nature, we began to ask why, if the no opened the space of the axiological, as we saw in Alain, it was the yes, in reality, that founded that space. The affirmative foundation of the axiological could take on two aspects, a *speculative* aspect (value of truth) and a *practical* aspect (the Good . . .). We tried to show that, in its speculative sense, this *yes* resisted two forms of negation that were also two forms of doubt. (1) *Skeptical doubt,* which, as we saw in some detail, refuses not only the right to affirmation but the right to opinion in general, whether affirmative or negative; it thus refuses *any right to speech* and makes the interrogative attitude the only safeguard from certainty. *Aphasia,* nonspeech, thus became the categorical imperative or rather the categorical prohibition through which one achieved those heights of wisdom called *ataraxia* and *adiaphoron.*

But, you can surmise, it is quite easy to show that this prohibition cannot sustain itself alone in its negativity. To indefinitely contradict every opinion, that is, every judgment, since it might be false and might fall into the traps of appearance, I must be inspired by a positive demand for truth and reality. It is by referring to a right to truth or to the right of truth that I can condemn error, hastiness, belief, appearance, and all nontruth in general. Without a kind of originary axiological adherence to the legitimacy of truth, it would not even be possible to reject opinion in general, judgment in general, as a de facto falling short of the truth. This primordial faith reveals itself in two guises:

1. The denunciations of the skeptics, the interrogative attitude of aphasia, implicitly refers to it and even manifests it in its purity.[2]

2. To the extent that skepticism presents itself as a philosophy, it presents itself as the bearer[3] of a truth, even if it is the truth of an impossible truth. The interrogative attitude is first of all a philosophical attitude, hence an attitude that I recommend and that I have the possibility, in principle, of teaching. This possibility of philosophical communication reveals a plane of possibility and a language that is deeper than that which one wants to strike with prohibition and aphasia. Aphasia is simply the most demanding mode of a fundamental *logos* through which every philosophy, and skeptical philosophy in particular, is initiated.

These denunciations are rather traditional, and so easy enough. They are in fact those that Pascal describes so well and at such length, especially when he shows the dogmatism inherent in all philosophical reason, including skeptical reason. In Fragment 375, he writes this single, seemingly enig-

2. In the manuscript the numbers "1" and "2" are encircled in red.

3. In the interlinear space above the word "bearer" appears the word "herald."

matic phrase, laced with a terrible irony: "The Pyrrhonian skeptic Arcesilaus, who becomes dogmatic again."[4] And he appeals to this same veracity when he writes the famous Fragment 395: "We have a powerlessness to prove that cannot be defeated by any dogmatism. We have an idea of truth that cannot be defeated by any pyrrhonism."[5]

So, easy enough . . .

The philosopher must therefore become aware of this ineradicable depth of truth as right and as norm. And after this becoming aware, he must subordinate his doubt and all negativity to it. This leads us to the second doubt, to the second speculative negation mentioned earlier: methodical doubt, which is a putting on the path toward truth. Here the schema is even easier. It is a matter of showing, by drawing on Descartes:

1. How doubt *leads to* certainty. This is the whole trajectory of the *Meditations*, which we studied very attentively with regard to the ontological argument.

2. How doubt not only *leads to* but also *proceeds from*, or at least *presupposes*, a number of certainties that are not representative ideas—marked by doubt—but the axioms of natural light: the axiom of causality, the axiom according to which the will to deceive is incompatible with the idea of God, etc. This "natural light," if it is the ether of thought, clearly shows that the *yes* is more *natural*, that is, more original, than the *no*, etc.

4. Blaise Pascal, *Pensées*, trans. T. S. Eliot (New York: E. P. Dutton & Co., 1958), fragment 375, 102; translation slightly modified; *Pensées et opuscules* (Paris: Hachette, 1946), fragment 375, 500. In the manuscript, after the quotation, there is a mark indicating an addition: "↔."

5. *Pensées*, Fragment 395, 107; *Pensées et opuscules*, Fragment 395, 508.

Easy enough . . . (more critical in the sciences [1] [illegible word][6] and [illegible word][7])

In the order of speculative axiology and truth, the *yes* is therefore prior to and irreducible to the *no*. This is also true in the order of practical axiology.

Here, I will propose the following schema:

1. Show that we *gain a degree of depth* by moving from speculative axiology to practical axiology.[8] For to want the true presupposes that the *true* is the *good*, that it is better to want the true than the nontrue, and that there is therefore already a practical and "moral" implication in the will to truth . . .

2. Show that all *practical nihilism is contradictory* and presupposes a faith in the Good in general. This is analogous to the schema established with regard to skepticism ([1] symmetrical since, as we have seen, it was presupposed by the previous demonstration).

I will give here three examples (offered as illustrations and not expounded for their own sake). I will indicate only the principle of development that they might allow.

1. *First idea and first example.*

Every will is a willing of the Good and, consequently, an affirmation of the Good. The idea that a will can be directed toward something other than this Good simply confuses the Good with one of its forms, whether it be pleasure, happi-

6. In the manuscript there is an illegible word that might be "tradition."

7. In the manuscript there is an illegible word that might be "geometry."

8. In the interlinear space the following was added in parentheses: "(avoid the static and symmetry)."

ness, or, on the contrary, malevolence, death, or suicide. To say that a homicidal or suicidal will is not a willing of the Good is to confuse the Good with one of its determined forms, with what one believes to be one of its forms within a particular system of values, and to forget that the person who kills or kills themself sees in death the Good. This means that Evil is not the opposite or the symmetrical counterpart of this general and formal Good, which is the mark of everything that is willed. The negation of any particular good in the apparent will for Evil is secondary and founded on a will for the Good. The *satanic* affirmation "I want Evil" or "I refuse the Good"[9] necessarily presupposes the metaphysical affirmation: I want the good or I find it good to want evil and to refuse the good. In other words, the absolute and ineluctable Good is not posited synthetically and in an a posteriori, contingent manner by some particular will; it is analytically a part of the concept of will and of action in general. Every act of will is an act of will toward the Good. I cannot want Evil in general.

That is why Socrates said that "no one is wicked willingly." It is why (first example) Socrates in the *Gorgias*, having just heard Callicles, following the speculative nihilism of the Sophists, Callicles, this ancestor of Nietzsche, try to show him that one can and even *must* want something other than the Good and justice, for example, power or selfish pleasure, Socrates has no problem showing Callicles that this so-called *will to power*, distinct from the Good, is merely the *powerlessness of the will to determine its true object*, which is the Good. For upon reflection, one would quickly realize that the will to power is also a will for the Good. The Good is always the will's last word; it is the truth of the will.

9. In the interlinear space the following was added: "no to the good."

Provided that it is not confused with some particular good, which may itself not be willed.

2. *Second idea and second example.* If one sometimes comes to believe that there exists a primordial negative will and a will for Evil, it is because of a *finitude* that prevents us from wanting and thinking the absolute Good and that causes us to confuse the Good "in general" with some particular good. It is because of this finitude that one believes the relativism of the good to be the last word on the matter, and that, as Montaigne says, "Some say that our good lies in virtue, others in sensual pleasure, others in conforming to nature; one man in knowledge; etc."[10] We believe we are rejecting the good and wanting evil because we do not think, due to a limitation, that wanting-evil is merely a determination and not a contradiction of a wanting-the-good, of a fundamental bene-volence.

Thus Malebranche[11] — who in this respect is also a Christian Plato, since he is an heir of that other Platonist, Saint Augustine — thus Malebranche insisted on reminding us that we could want only the Good in general, that is, the absolute Good, that is, God; and that, as a result, every will, whatever its determined and accidental object, and even if it appears to be evil, actually proceeds from a will for the Good, hence from a will for God, hence from a love of God. And if we are attached to particular goods, those which precisely bear the name of evils, as in, for example, the drunkard's passion and

10. Michel de Montaigne, "Apology for Raymond Sebond," in *The Complete Essays*, trans. Donald M. Frame (Stanford, CA: Stanford University Press, 1958), 435; "Apologie de Raimond Sebond," in *Les essais*, ed. Albert Thibaudet (Paris: Gallimard, Bibliothèque de la Pléiade, 1946). Derrida shortens the quotation from Montaigne.

11. In the interlinear space an addition indicates here: "second example."

love for wine, it is because our finite understanding is incapable of determining the true object of infinite will, which is God. Through the bottle of wine, it is God that the drunkard adores, though he cannot know this. For when I believe I am rejecting God, it is still God that I am affirming. . . . The will is always, necessarily, a will for the indeterminate good in general. Let us note in passing that, since we, as finite beings, cannot possess this infinite will, it is God who, through us, wills and loves Himself with a pure love.[12] Easy enough.

Thus, the affirmation of value seems to be the form of a fundamental yes in relation to which all negation appears secondary, derivative, and dependent.

3. *This leads us to the third idea and the third example.*

This affirmation of value seems even more radical than the affirmation and positing of being. To posit being, is it not necessary to want it, to want to posit it and to think it? Is this not necessary insofar as it is better that there should be being rather than nonbeing? Is not the affirmation of value what remains when nihilism has been taken to its extreme, when it has denied everything right up to the existence of God?

This is what allows *Lagneau*,[13] in his famous *Course on God* (Lagneau being Alain's teacher in the lycée), to say that one must go through a proof of God's nonexistence to understand what God is,[14] that is, to understand that God *is not* but that He presents Himself in the form of absolute

12. In the interlinear space the following was added: "The no = reduced to the level of the infinite."

13. In the interlinear space above "Lagneau" an addition indicates: "third example."

14. In the margin, Derrida adds a quotation from Lagneau in parentheses: "('Atheism is the salt that prevents belief in God from being corrupted')." Jules Lagneau, *Célèbres leçons et fragments* (Paris: Presses Universitaires de France, 1950), 231.

value; that without this God, this absolute value, one would have to stop thinking, willing, and turn towards nothingness and chaos.[15]

So, after having thus reached the most fundamental level of the *yes*, after having purified it of everything that was not it, and shown that it was the ultimate foundation of thought, discourse, and will, and the first word of philosophy, we are left, in a third and final major section, with the following dual question: If the *yes* is primary and irreducible, what is the meaning and origin of the no? Why is there negation, and why is Alain's "to think is to say no" not in contradiction with this more fundamental *yes*? Second, *second question*, which, you will see, we will have to address along the way: is the axiological affirmation, the yes to absolute value, *prior* and *primary*, as Lagneau thinks, or is it dependent on a more radical ontological affirmation? And if so, what is this radical ontological affirmation?

The question of the origin of negation is, in many respects, a modern question. Of course, negation and negativity in general, we must not forget, are already problematized by Plato, where the negative appears in the dual forms of the *apeiron* (the indefinite—indeterminate) and the exclusion of determinations, the alterity of ideas. This is the problem of alterity and of nonbeings in the *Sophist*. (Thus, indeterminability and exclusion.) To be sure, negativity is also taken into account by classical rationalists. But negativity is always thought of as absence and privation, as a lack in what

15. In the manuscript there is a mark indicating an addition: "↔," followed, in parentheses, by: "(We will return to this.)"

is not it, that is, a lack in what is. It is only beginning with Kant, who, particularly in his *Essay to Introduce the Concept of Negative Magnitude into Philosophy* (1763), shows that negation is subtraction, absence, lack, etc., only in a logical or discursive sense, but that as soon as one moves from the logical to the real, one finds that there are conflicts of force, thus "negative magnitudes" that are no longer merely by default the shadow of a positive magnitude but another magnitude just as real. (Note that the brilliant Bossuet had already observed this: unhappy ≠ not happy, unjust ≠ not just.)

It was Hegel who then took seriously the labor of the negative and thereby completed the movement that led us out of a tradition[16] for which negation was *fundamentally* the impossible or the unthinkable, or in any case, that which, as such, had no hold on being . . .

It is against the backdrop of this revival that the question of the origin and meaning of negation reemerged with such acuity at the end of the last century. It has not lost any of its urgency since.

This question can be posed, and was indeed first posed, in its logical form. How is a negative judgment possible? What am I doing when I say X is not Y, when I say, "the sky is not blue"?[17]

The first temptation is obviously to think that such a judgment presents no originality and is merely a simple affirmation; the affirmation of a discordance between the subject and the attribute. I posit the sky, I posit blue, and I posit the discordance, the incongruence of blue with the sky. From a logical perspective, it seems that the negative lacks

16. In the manuscript, "of a tradition" replaces "of the logic of the useless and of classical ontology," which is crossed out.

17. Following this paragraph there is an addition: "A few historical elements → development of the dossier."

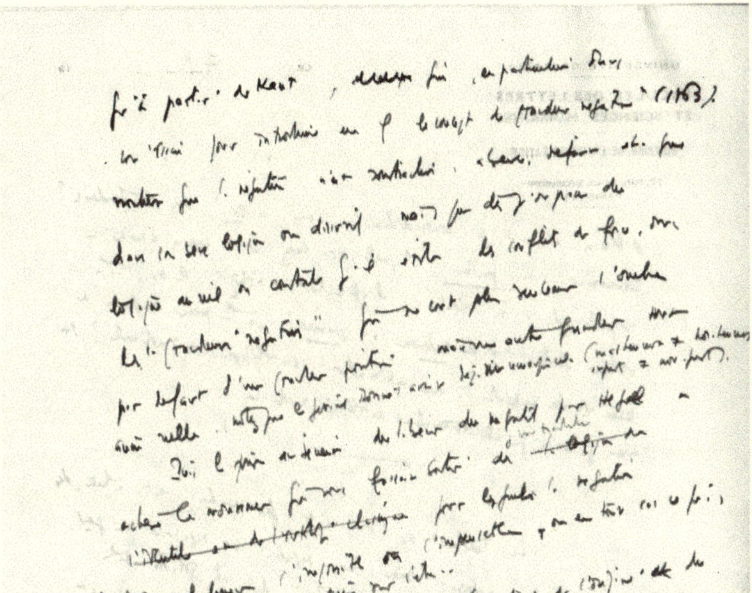

Figure 3. A page of Derrida's handwritten manuscript, corresponding to page 46 of the printed text.

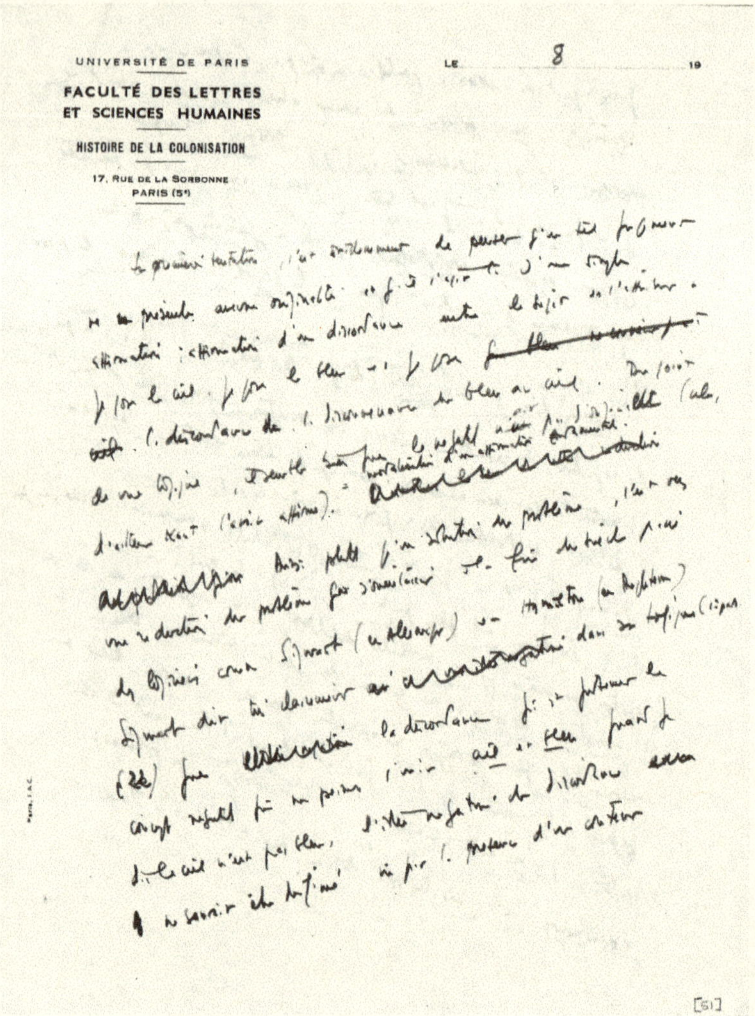

UNIVERSITÉ DE PARIS

LE 8 19

FACULTÉ DES LETTRES
ET SCIENCES HUMAINES

HISTOIRE DE LA COLONISATION

17, RUE DE LA SORBONNE
PARIS (5e)

[51]

Figure 4. A page of Derrida's handwritten manuscript, corresponding to page(s) 46 and 49 of the printed text.

originality (indeed, Kant had asserted this) = the modalization of a fundamental affirmation.

Thus, rather than looking for a solution to the problem, logicians like Sigwart (in Germany) and Hamilton (in England) at the end of the last century looked toward a reduction of the problem. Sigwart clearly states in his *Logic* (Part 1, § 22) that the discordance, which is precisely the negative concept that allows us to unite *sky* and *blue* when I say the sky is not blue, the negative idea of discordance can be defined neither by the presence of a positive mental content nor by the absence of such content, because to think of A as absent is first to think it and thus to have it present to the mind.

This means that, strictly speaking, pure absence is not thinkable and negation only ever affects a presence, the presence of a particular sign: the possible, the elsewhere, the past, etc.

Hamilton says the same thing (*Logic* III, 216): "Hence it also follows, that there is no negation conceivable without the concomitant conception of an affirmation, for we cannot deny a thing to exist, without having a notion of the existence which is denied."[18]

In other words, in both negative judgments—copulative or attributive on the one hand, "the sky is not blue," existential on the other hand, "there is no sky"—negation would merely be a modality or complication of affirmation; it would be a species of the genus affirmation. It would be there to correct a possible and erroneous affirmation (if I were tempted to say, for example: the sky is blue when it is gray) by means of another affirmation. This is why, consider-

18. William Hamilton, *Lectures on Metaphysics and Logic* (Edinburgh and London: William Blackwood and Sons, 1866), 3:216.

ing only the logical plane, Kant said that: "From the point of view of our knowledge in general . . . the peculiar function of negative propositions is simply to prevent error."[19]

This explanation concerns the *form of negative judgment* and its *classifications within the category of judgments*, but even if it were satisfactory and its orientation correct, it would tell us nothing about *the origin of negation*. How and why does one come to complicate and modalize the primordial, fundamental affirmation?[20]

It is this *problem of origin* that Bergson, in a famous text in the *Revue philosophique* of 1906 and reprinted in *Creative Evolution* (1907), tries to solve, in a way that is at once classical and revolutionary. Classical because it starts from the unity and fullness of being. Revolutionary in that it demonstrates that only the identification of being with duration allows access to the fullness of being and so offers the solution to the problem of negation.

Let us try to *repeat* this Bergsonian schema, which is fundamentally the same as the one he applies to the idea of disorder and to the idea of the possible.

To ascribe any kind of originality and ineluctable gravity to negation, negation must somehow find its origin in a

19. Derrida here seems to be quoting Henri Bergson, who is himself quoting Kant, in *Creative Evolution*, trans. Arthur Mitchell (New York: Henry Holt and Company, 1913), 287n1; *L'évolution créatrice* (Paris: Felix Alcan, 1907), 312n3: "Kant, *Critique of Pure Reason*, 2nd ed., 737: 'From the point of view of our knowledge in general . . . the peculiar function of negative propositions is simply to prevent error.' Cf. Christian Sigwart, *Logik, oder die Lehre vom Erkennen und Beweisen*, 2nd ed., vol. 1 (Leipzig: W. Friedrich, 1882), 150 ff." In the manuscript, after the quotation, there are three words in parentheses that are crossed out: "(cited by Sigwart)."

20. In the interlinear space the following is added in parentheses: "why discordance-error?"

nothingness, thus in something like, if not a being, at least a presence, a positivity of nothingness.[21]

Now, Bergson tells us, nothingness is an *illusion* constructed out of action. Every action is[22] in search of something, an object of which we are deprived, and it aims to create something that does not exist. It thus presupposes a kind of partial unreality, but this partial unreality is merely the absence of a presence that is being sought.[23] By substantivizing this absence—this partial unreality—and generalizing the concept, I create the illusion of nothingness.

It is therefore crucial to rid oneself of this idea of nothingness since it has been the hidden driving force behind all classical metaphysics. It is a sort of *myth of homo faber* that would have thus misled all pre-Bergsonian philosophy. For when one asks the question: *How to deny that something exists? Why is there something rather than nothing?*, a question that begins with *Who am I* and *From where do I derive my essence and existence*; these questions presuppose *nothingness*. Starting from this *presumption*, existence appears as a conquest over nothingness. Being supervenes upon nothingness; it comes to it subsequently and in addition. Nothingness is, Bergson says, in a series of images: the *receptacle*, the *carpet*, the *substratum* of being. And even if one admits that, *in fact*, the emptiness does not *preexist* the fullness, that in the glass of water the emptiness of the glass *container* is contemporaneous with the fullness of the water *contained*, one nonetheless wants, *by right* [*en droit*], *juridically*, for the emptiness to precede the full: the glass of water must first be, by right, empty before it can be filled.

Thus, says Bergson, in another image (still very expres-

21. In the manuscript there is a mark indicating an addition: "↔."
22. In the interlinear space there is the addition: "presupposition."
23. In the manuscript there is a mark indicating an addition: "↔."

sive, even if [two illegible words][24] does not mention it[25]): "I cannot get rid of the idea that the full is an embroidery on the canvas of the empty, that being is superimposed on nothing, and that in the idea of 'nothing' there is *less* than in that of 'something.'"[26] All the *mystery* comes from there.

Well, this *mystery* is a *mystification*, and the idea of nothingness is a *pseudo-idea* that must be exorcised.

What do we do when we claim to *represent nothingness*? Well, we can 1. imagine it;

2. conceive it.

When, through *imagination* (in Bergson's sense [illegible word][27]) I annihilate an external object as a whole or the totality of possible external objects (by closing my eyes . . .), I no longer perceive anything but internal objects; and when, conversely, I annihilate all internal images, I no longer perceive anything but external objects.

"The absence of one consists, at bottom [says Bergson], in the presence of the other. But, [Bergson adds, and here is the deception and the mechanism of illusion] from the fact that two relative nothingnesses are imaginable *in turn*, we wrongly conclude that they are imaginable *together*: a conclusion the absurdity of which must be obvious, for we cannot imagine a nothingness without perceiving, at least confusedly, that we are imagining it, consequently that we

24. In the manuscript there are two illegible words that might be "his point,"

25. In the manuscript, "does not mention it" replaces "is not explained," which is crossed out.

26. Bergson, *Creative Evolution*, 276; *L'évolution créatrice*, 299. Italics present in the original and underlined by Derrida. Bergson's original ends with the phrase "Hence all the mystery" ("*De là tout le mystère*"), which Derrida paraphrases.

27. In the manuscript there is an illegible word that might be "therefore."

are acting, that we are thinking, and therefore that something still subsists."[28]

Imagination of nothingness: Thus, a reduction of *alternative succession* to *simultaneity*.

But if I cannot *imagine* nothingness, can I not think it (cf. Descartes's chiliagon)? One can always think the abolition of an object, and if I extend this intellectual operation to infinity, nothingness will be the *limit concept* of this operation. But it is precisely this passage to the limit that Bergson finds contradictory and absurd, intellectually speaking. The idea of abolition and destruction can have as a correlate only a part of the whole, and not the whole itself. The idea of an abolition of the Whole has the same characteristics as that of a square circle: it is no longer an idea but a *word*. The whole is what cannot be abolished; it is that in which any partial abolition is possible. Absolute emptiness does not therefore exist. Emptiness is always the determined place of a partial absence, but the absent object is always replaced by another present object. At bottom, there is in being never destruction or *abolition* but *substitution*. There is thus absence only for a being capable of *recollection*—recollection of the object replaced by another and which seems absent—or capable of *expectation*, *desire*, *preference*, hence of *disappointment* [déception]. The full thus always succeeds the full, and without regret or desire, without any absence. "The representation of emptiness is always a representation which is full and which resolves itself on analysis into two positive ele-

28. Bergson, *Creative Evolution*, 279; *L'évolution créatrice*, 302. Derrida underlines the note number, adds the words in brackets, and omits the word "exclusive" from the first sentence of the quotation, which reads: "in the exclusive presence of the other."

ments: the idea, distinct or confused, of a substitution, and the feeling, experienced or imagined, of a desire or regret."

Thus, paradoxically, nothing is not less than the whole, the empty is not less than the full, and the *negated* object is not any less than the idea of the *posited* or the *affirmed* object. For, as Bergson says: "The idea of the object 'not existing' is necessarily the idea of the object '*existing*' with, *in addition*, the representation of an exclusion of this object by the actual reality taken in block."[29]

Bergson encounters here the following objection, which allows him to refine his description of the genesis of this negative judgment.

Here is the objection: To be sure, I can in fact, in actuality, only replace one thing with another, and it is nonsense to speak of *real* nothingness. But can I not *ideally* abolish the thing and think its nothingness by means of a *negative* judgment, by denying the blue of the sky or by denying the existence of a particular object?

In Bergson's view, such a hypothesis is the source of all errors because it assumes that the *no* is symmetrical with the *yes* in terms of possibility, and thus that the Nothing is symmetrical with the whole. But it is nothing of the sort. We have already seen why this symmetry is impossible. Here is an additional reason.

Affirmation, says Bergson, is a *complete* intellectual act, while negation is merely a mutilated affirmation, only half of an intellectual act that consists in setting aside a possible affirmation without substituting another for it.

29. Bergson, *Creative Evolution*, 286; *L'évolution créatrice*, 310. Derrida's emphasis.

Thus, when I say, "this table is black," I perceive what I affirm and affirm what I perceive. My judgment is based directly on a perception.

Conversely, when I say, "this table is not white," I do not perceive the nonwhite, I do not perceive the absence of white, but I still perceive black, or red, or yellow.

That is why it is an incomplete act: I set aside an affirmation (the table is white) without completing and without saying what should be substituted for the false or possible judgment . . .[30]

In the negative judgment, it is thus not the table itself that I am judging when I say, "the table is not white." I am judging another judgment[31] that would be claiming that the table is white. I am judging a judgment, not the table. This allows Bergson to say: "Negation, therefore, differs from affirmation . . . in that it is an affirmation of the *second degree*: it affirms something of an affirmation which itself affirms something of an object."[32]

To affirm something of an affirmation is, thus, to respond in some sense by anticipation to an affirmation that one wants to correct, overturn, or reject. This is why negation presupposes that a dialogue has been established between an other [*autrui*] and myself, between myself and myself. Bergson was not the first to point out the constant complicity between negativity and dialectic when he said that negation has a pedagogical function and that it presupposes a "*begin-*

30. In the manuscript there is a mark indicating an addition: "↔."

31. In the interlinear space there is an addition that might be: "possible (virtual)."

32. Bergson, *Creative Evolution*, 288; *L'évolution créatrice*, 313. The emphasis here comes from Derrida, who also omits a few words from the quotation.

ning of society":[33] it is there to teach, to denounce error, to warn, and if it is in essence *dialectical*, it points more to the dialectic *of master and disciple* than to that *of master and slave*.

But the healthy pedagogical function secretes illusion when logical formalism is taken seriously, when the negative judgment is considered to be symmetrical to the affirmative judgment, when the words of conventional language are taken for things, and when logical and discursive negativity is substantivized and taken for a real nothingness, a possible being of nonbeing.

Negation is therefore the product of language, intelligence, action, and society. As Bergson says, p. 316, "Suppose all this has been abolished" and you eliminate every "wish to deny."[34] This is all too obvious, and from the start. So as not to see in this Bergsonian thesis the most trivial and derisory of truisms, one must not forget that one does not eliminate everything, and particularly not what is essential about the mind, quite to the contrary, by eliminating or transcending language, intelligence, and action. This entire critique

33. Bergson, *Creative Evolution*, 288; *L'évolution créatrice*, 312. Derrida's emphasis.

34. Bergson, *Creative Evolution*, 292; *L'évolution créatrice*, 316. Derrida is paraphrasing the following quotation from Bergson: "Suppose language fallen into disuse, society dissolved, every intellectual initiative, every faculty of self-reflection and of self-judgment atrophied in man: the dampness of the ground will subsist none the less, capable of inscribing itself automatically in sensation and of sending a vague idea to the deadened intellect. The intellect will still affirm, in implicit terms. And consequently, neither distinct concepts, nor words, nor the desire of spreading the truth, nor that of bettering oneself, are of the very essence of the affirmation. But this passive intelligence, mechanically keeping steps with experience, neither anticipating nor following the course of the real, would have no wish to deny."

aims, on the contrary, to restore the rights of metadiscursive intuition and the being of duration in its fullness.

Indeed, after having been referred by the pseudo-idea of nothingness to its origin in logical-discursive negation, Bergson returns to this nothingness to show that the question "Why does something exist?" makes no sense. It was this question, this pseudo-question born from a pseudo-idea, that seemed to pose problems for a philosophy of duration since it presumed a static being that emerged all at once, by a sort of revolution upon itself of a nothingness that supposedly preceded it.

> This long analysis [Bergson writes (p. 322/323)] has been necessary to show that a self-sufficient reality is not necessarily a reality foreign to duration. If we pass (consciously or unconsciously) through the idea of nothingness in order to reach that of Being, the Being to which we come is a logical or mathematical essence, therefore non-temporal. And, consequently, a static conception of the real is forced on us: everything appears given once for all, in eternity. But we must accustom ourselves to think Being directly, without making a detour, without first appealing to the phantom of nothingness which interposes itself between it and us. We must try *to see in order to see*, and no longer to see in order to act. Then the Absolute is revealed very near us and, in a certain measure, in us. It is of psychological and not of mathematical nor logical essence. It lives with us. Like us, but in certain aspects infinitely more concentrated and more gathered up in itself, *it endures.*[35]

35. *Creative Evolution*, 298–99; *L'évolution créatrice*, 323. Derrida's emphasis.

The Bergsonian movement of thought suggests, in its force and depth, that one should not be too quick to dismiss the notion that negativity has no place in a philosophy of intuition and immediacy, which is always a philosophy of fullness.[36] It is always through discourse that nothingness comes to being and that the Absolute separates from itself. Nonbeing and discourse are interconnected, and the Absolute seen from being has, by right, only silence as its element. As Birault says in a very fine article on "Heidegger and the Thought of Finitude" (R. I. Ph.), a difficult and subtle but very rich article, "to speak is always to speak against God" and "discourse is the true beginning of atheism."[37]

The point here is thus not to "criticize" Bergson. In fact, *criticizing* a philosopher is a deplorable gesture that makes no sense and necessarily operates within the space of unintelligence. What we can do here is repeat Bergsonism by posing three questions on the basis of it.

1. Can we say that, in terms of judgment and descriptive language, the dissymmetry between affirmation and negation is the final word? And that the symmetry is necessarily broken in favor of affirmation, which would be primary and at a deeper level?

2. Is discourse in the deepest sense of the term necessarily the degradation, the accidental aspect of a thought directed towards action; a pejorative meaning that resonates with the sense of negation?

36. In the interlinear space, a phrase is added that could be: "That is to say, affirmation of being in all philosophy, and particularly in that of value."

37. Henri Birault, "Heidegger et la pensée de la finitude," *Revue internationale de philosophie* 14, no. 52(2) (1960): 140.

3. Can we determine, around this critique of negation, the essence of absolute Being as *psychological*? "Then the Absolute is revealed very near us and, in a certain measure, in us. It is of psychological essence . . ."[38]

In answering these three questions, we will conclude next time by referring to:

1. Lachelier, who criticizes the alleged logical dissymmetry discussed by Bergson.

2. Husserl, who describes, beneath the psychological origin and within predicative judgment, a transcendental origin of negation, presenting a schema that somewhat resembles Bergson's but that ≠ [illegible word][39] ≠ psychological.

3. Sartre, who sees in negation an extreme pre-judication and links negativity to the structure of the for-itself.

4. Heidegger, finally, for whom[40] the thought of being presupposes, in anxiety, for example, the nihilation [*néantisation*] of the totality of beings.

38. Bergson, *Creative Evolution*, 298–99; *L'évolution créatrice*, 323.

39. In the manuscript there is an illegible word that might be "predicative."

40. In the manuscript there are several words that have been crossed out: "the origin of negation cannot be found in any being, not in consciousness, not in the for-itself."

Fourth Session

"To think is to say no." (4)

We had, recall, reached the *third* and *final* major part of our discussion when the definition of the fundamental axiological *yes* of faith led us to question the origin and meaning of negation. If the axiological *yes* of *Faith*, as we had defined it with Alain, indeed resists, as we have seen, (1) skeptical doubt and methodical doubt in the order of speculative axiology, and (2) even more profoundly, practical nihilism in the order of moral axiology, as we also saw in three stages with Plato, Malebranche, and Lagneau; if this *yes* was, then, so irreducibly primordial, how did it become complicated by negation? And was not the axiological yes dependent, despite everything, on an ontological *yes*?

In following out these questions, we were led to define the position of logicians such as Sigwart and Hamilton, who, without posing the question of origin, see negation, at the level of constituted judgment, as a mere species of the genus affirmation.

The *question of origin* really came to be posed with Bergson, whose description we analyzed at length. At the end of this analysis, we raised a number of questions that we will take up today in order to conclude.

1. First, can we simply accept Bergson's demonstration

regarding the *dissymmetry* between affirmative and negative judgments?[1] According to Bergson, you will recall, the negative judgment is an *incomplete*, *secondary*, and *dialectical* judgment:

— *incomplete*, because it says what something is not without saying what it is;
— *secondary*, since it concerns an affirmative judgment that it rejects and not an object that it qualifies;[2]
— *dialectical*, because it has a pedagogical and social function of denunciation or warning when faced with the other's error, who is found to be mistaken.

Now, one might rightly wonder whether, with regard to *judgment*, the predicative attitude, the attitude of someone saying, "this is that" or "this is not that," we cannot discover the same characteristics of *incompleteness*, *secondariness*, and *dialecticity* in the affirmative judgment, so that the symmetry would thereby be reestablished.

That is what people like Lachelier and Goblot think. When I say, "the table is white," I experience the necessity not only to perceive it naively and for myself but to say it, to utter a judgment. And this is because I implicitly experience the possibility of a symmetrical negative judgment. If I say, "the table is white," it is not only because I see it as such, but because *one* could say the opposite. This "*one*" could be anyone, a subject in general, the disciple we talked about last week, or even myself a moment before or a moment after . . .

The affirmative *judgment* is, insofar as it is language, and

1. In the manuscript this numbering will not continue.

2. In the manuscript there is the following addition: "judgment → judgment / again [*encore*] → [illegible word]."

already from its first and most spontaneous utterance,[3] in a dialogical situation. It is, like any judgment, a *proposition*, something that one puts forward, in advance, something that one advances toward another person who can assess it, that is, another who, I always already presume, can say or want to say the opposite. An affirmative judgment is always a *thesis*, and I would not feel the need to utter, to formulate a thesis were I not doing so *against* its opposite, against its possible contestation,[4] against an *antithesis* that I cross out, precisely, in the affirmative judgment. You see that the reference to the negative judgment also haunts the affirmative judgment, whose thesis is always linked to the hypothesis of a contestation. Thus, one can say of the affirmative judgment what Bergson said of the negative judgment: it is as much a judgment on a possible judgment as it is a judgment on an object. It is therefore just as secondary and dialectical as the negative judgment. In the end, the characteristics defined by Bergson are those of the judicative attitude in general and of objective language in general.

The principle of this reversal is to be found, as I was saying a moment ago, in Lachelier. He goes further and attacks the critique of the very idea of nothingness, which was of a piece with Bergson's description of the negative judgment.

Indeed, it is one of two things, says Lachelier[5] in a very

3. In the manuscript the word "spontaneous [*primesautière*]" was later circled and seems to have been placed by means of an arrow after the word "utterance." The original order has been retained here for the coherence of the sentence.

4. [While the French edition has *constatation* (observation) here, the manuscript seems to say "contestation" (*contestation*).—Trans.]

5. André Lalande, *Vocabulaire technique et critique de la philosophie*, 6th ed. (Paris: Presses Universitaires de France, 1950). The passage by Jules Lachelier quoted here by Derrida appears in the entry on "Nothingness."

brief remark in the Lalande dictionary,[6] which I will try to develop here: either the mind and thought are something, or else they are nothing. If they are nothing, the case is clear; the negation of something existent or of the totality of existents is merely a dream, a sort of "heroic" phantasm by which I would attempt to grant myself a demi-divinity[7] by de-creating, in an illusory and derisory manner, through the empty image or concept, an existence that does just fine without me.[8] It would be a kind of hallucination *in reverse* where I would believe I could deprive myself of the real, whereas simple hallucination consists in giving oneself the imaginary.

But if the mind and thought are something (and Bergson would deny this less than others), they must be taken seriously when they refuse or refrain from positing existence. It is a question of their philosophical freedom, and the being of the mind is freedom.

Here is what Lachelier writes:

> If the mind and thought are something, and if *to exist* means to be posited by the mind, the mind can, with the same freedom, posit any being or refuse to posit anything (or at least conceive of itself by abstraction as positing nothing, conceive its own freedom outside of any actual exercise of that freedom). Mr. Bergson's remark is singularly profound and perfectly accurate from the standpoint of his realism; but it turns against that very realism. The idea of nothingness implies

6. Derrida subsequently places the two words "Lalande dictionary" in parentheses.

7. In the interlinear space above "demi-," the word "pseudo" is added.

8. In the margin of the manuscript there is an addition that might be: "Being is not moved by our negation."

and verifies the idea of "freedom" (in my sense of the word and not in his).[9]

Let us go back over this text.

If the mind and thought are something, and if . . .

1[10]—*to exist is to be posited by the mind*. To say that to exist is to be posited by the mind—a spiritualist thesis, needless to say—does not mean, for that would be rather naive, that existence depends *in its reality, in its flesh*, in its existentiality, on a creative decision of the mind. To say that to exist is to be posited by the mind means that existence can be recognized in its meaning as existence, that it can be posited *as* existent, as such, that it exists "as such," only by an act of the mind. This table indeed exists on its own, without any act of the mind positing it in its being, and this is precisely what *to exist* means. But it can have its meaning as existent, it can be *said* to exist, only through an act of the mind without which its existence would never appear and would never ground any logos or any philosophy. Now, in order for the mind to be, as we have just seen, *responsible* for this act, the act must be free. If it is free, it can equally well posit or not posit existence in something like an *epoché* (in both the skeptical and phenomenological senses of the word), this *epoché* revealing the highest possibility, that is, the highest freedom, of the mind.

That is why Lachelier wrote, "if to exist means to be posited by the mind, the mind can, with the *same*[11] *freedom*, posit any being or refuse to posit anything (or at least conceive itself by abstraction as positing nothing, conceive

9. Jules Lachelier, "Nothingness," in Lalande, *Vocabulaire technique et critique de la philosophie*, Derrida's emphasis.

10. In the manuscript this numbering will not continue.

11. Derrida underlines the word "same" several times in the manuscript.

its own freedom outside of any actual exercise of that freedom)."[12] In the end, the imagination through which I am able to remove from something its meaning of presence or of existence—we saw this with Sartre—the imagination by which I can, in principle, suspend the thesis of existence regarding the totality of the world, this imagination, this fantasy, is the true seriousness of the mind, which thereby presents itself to itself in the original and authentic sense of its power. It is thus through negation or the thought of nothingness that the mind authenticates itself as freedom. Without this, without this negating freedom—and this is what is important—affirmation itself would be impossible and without any value. When I say, "the table is white," I am not performing a "natural" gesture in the form of a conditioned reflex, a bodily desire, or the extension of a simple physiological perception. For my affirmative judgment to have value as truth, I must have been free to choose in favor of the truth, and I must have been able to say something other than what I say. This is the case of attributive judgment.

The same applies to the judgment of existence, as when I say, "the table exists." If I say, "the table exists," I am implying that I could think and posit the nonexistence of the table. Bergson made use of the Kantian critique of the ontological argument in a strange way. Claiming to be relying on Kant, he said the following, in a way reversing Kant's proposition: positing A as existent or as nonexistent changes nothing about the concept of A (about its definition).[13] Thus, thinking A as nonexistent is the same as thinking it as existent. I do not think anything other than A when I deny existence to A. The negation or the "nihilation" [*néan-*

12. Jules Lachelier, "Nothingness," in Lalande, *Vocabulaire technique et critique de la philosophie*.

13. In the manuscript there is a mark indicating an addition: "↔."

tisation] is therefore illusory. For to think is to think about the existent. This is a curious interpretation of Kantianism, which ultimately ends up in a position radically opposed to Kant's and places existence within the concept by using the argument that nonexistence does not modify the concept. For Kant, in fact, neither existence nor nonexistence is in the concept, and both require acts of positing or nonpositing that are entirely originary and extralogical.

When Lachelier thus says that Bergson is correct from the standpoint of his realism but that the critique of the idea of nothingness turns against his realism, he means this: It is no doubt consistent with a realism to say that every thought must first be an intuition of the existent, and that being is always the *undeniable*, but this thesis turns against realism in that it does not give freedom its due. For it is only from this freedom, as we have seen, that the affirmation of being and its "undeniability" gains value and meaning. We return to Lagneau's idea and to the dependence of the ontological affirmation of being on the axiological affirmation of value. True realism, that is, philosophical realism, the kind that is *thought*, that is *critical* and not naive or animal, presupposes with respect to the totality of being a freedom, and thus a power of negation. This allows Lachelier to conclude: "The idea of nothingness implies and verifies the idea of 'freedom,'"[14] and to add: "in my sense of the word and not in Bergson's."[15]

Because, of course, freedom for Bergson is not this abstract possibility of choosing between contraries, something he criticizes in the final part of the *Essay on the Immediate*

14. Lachelier, "Nothingness."

15. Ibid. Derrida changes the original quotation, which reads "(in my sense of the word and not in his)."

Data of Consciousness,[16] but the becoming [illegible word][17] in pure, concrete, and lived duration.

It is easy to see how Bergson might escape Lachelier's critique. He would do so by conceding that, at the level of judgment and language—in the deepest sense of the word—there is still symmetry between the *yes* and the *no*, but that, since every judgment and every language always *ultimately* refers to a pre-predicative and silent perception, the symmetry is here again broken in favor of a primordial affirmation. Note that he does not do this explicitly: His entire analysis is developed at the level of judgment, and it is the priority of judgment and affirmative language that he claims to demonstrate.

Goblot does do this, when, in his *Treatise on Logic*, he starts by adopting Lachelier's critique and then concludes that it is *perception* and not *judgment* that contains this irreducible and primitive *assertion*.

Here is what he writes on page 167 of his *Treatise*:

> Let us first note that affirmative judgments can also be expressed by means of a modal formulation: "You would be wrong to deny or doubt that . . ." The dialectical and polemical character—"pedagogical and social," says Mr. Bergson—of negative judgments also applies to many affirmative judgments. Affirmation can be a protest against a possible negation; it, too, can "target someone and not something."
>
> *The distinction must be placed elsewhere.*[18] Either

16. Henri Bergson, *Time and Free Will: An Essay on the Immediate Data of Consciousness*, trans. F. L. Pogson (London: George Allen & Unwin Ltd, 1910); *Essai sur les données immédiates de la conscience* (Paris: Presses Universitaires de France, 1948 [1927]).

17. In the manuscript there is an illegible word that might be "other."

18. Derrida's emphasis.

> the judgment, whether affirmative or negative, is the response to a questioning, the result of an examination, the end of a debate, the conclusion of a doubt. In this case, the *yes* presupposes the possibility of the *no*, just as the *no* presupposes the possibility of the *yes*. Or else the judgment is made immediately, without doubt or prior examination; it is not a "*response*"[19] but a piece of information that simply appears and was not asked for. It can thus only be affirmative. This is the case of the assertion implied in every perception.[20]

What is still troubling in Goblot is that he still makes perception a sort of judgment, following a rather classic intellectualism. Which risks becoming somewhat incoherent because every judgment, perceptual or not, breaks the immediacy of the primary assertion. Thus, one must go [illegible word][21] before judgment in order to give this thesis all its force. We will then see that, even if, in the end, the yes still comes first, there is already a possible negation before judgment and before language.

This is what Husserl shows in § 21 of *Erfahrung und Urteil* (*Experience and Judgment*).[22] This book was put together by one of Husserl's students, Landgrebe, based on a manuscript

19. Derrida's emphasis and addition of quotation marks.

20. Edmond Goblot, *Traité de logique* (Paris: Librairie Armand Colin, 1918), 167.

21. In the manuscript there is an illegible word that might be "resolutely."

22. Edmund Husserl, *Experience and Judgment: Investigations in a Genealogy of Logic*, trans. James S. Churchill and Karl Ameriks (Evanston, IL: Northwestern University Press, 1973), §21, 87–101; *Erfahrung und Urteil: Untersuchungen zur Genealogie der Logik* (Hamburg: Claassen und Goverts, 1948).

from 1919, and its development was attentively supervised by Husserl until 1938.

Husserl's description, whose conclusions, in their basic outline, could be aligned with Bergson's, has two advantages over Bergson's.

1. It goes back down to the depths of the pre-predicative experience that underlies judgment.[23]

2. Although it makes reference to *disappointment*,[24] it is not a psychological analysis but a transcendental one. As you know, for Husserl the psychological is not, as it is for Bergson, the ultimate reference and ultimate reality. The psychological is something intramundane, constituted by a transcendental subject and "reduced" by the *epoché*. The Husserlian analysis is thus, here, free from the metaphysics or speculative presumption that, in the Bergsonian critique of negation, makes the psychological the deepest level of being, the very essence of the real. You recall the text quoted on this subject.

For Husserl, every judgment is the product of a secondary activity. The ultimate ground of judgment is a passive belief, a prejudicative, thus precritical, naive adhesion to things that are always pregiven to us in some way. This belief, this passive and naive adhesion to the pregiven world, is what Husserl calls *doxa*. Without having, as in Greek philosophy, a pejorative sense, *doxa* nonetheless means, as it does in Greek philosophy, and in Plato in particular, in opposition to episteme, the prejudging, prelogical, pre-epistemological adhesion to what appears, to what is given to me. Of course, with Plato → shadow. With Husserl, no metaphysics. It is beings [*l'étant*] that are thus pregiven to me even before I

23. In the manuscript the following is added and framed by a line: "Goblot and Bergson [illegible word] perception."

24. In the manuscript the words "and to doubt" are crossed out.

judge them and say *this* is *that*. Even before reflecting and judging, I know that the world is there, that there are things that exist outside of me and that this pregiven world is what all affirmation, all truth, all science refer to. It is to doxa that all *episteme* refers. This pregiven, which is lived before judgment, is the weight of things in the "life-world" and thus the measure and gravity of all philosophical or scientific utterances; this prejudicative *yes* is therefore a first and irreducible certainty that escapes, as such, all negativity. In particular, all hallucination and all imagination presuppose, in principle, this doxical certainty of what is always pregiven in perception. You see how far we are from Alain's critique of belief. Without there necessarily being, however, a contradiction here between Alain and Husserl. Alain's belief was defined in terms of judgment, as hasty judgment, as imprudent and naive language about appearance. Alain's belief was a judgment, a *pre-judice*,[25] that is, a "judged-in-advance," by presumption, while original doxa in Husserl is prejudication, meaning it conditions and precedes judgment, it is the pregiven on which the logical activity of judgment will operate.

Now, how will negation appear on the basis of this passive *doxa*? How will this primary certainty get modified into negation?[26] Here too, as with Bergson, through something like "a disappointed anticipation" (p. 94)[27]: "The interest taken

25. In the margin of the manuscript, Derrida adds and underlines "of the sort [*du genre*]," connecting it with a line to "pre-judice [*pré-jugé*]" in the body of the text.

26. In the manuscript Derrida adds and underlines: "Not by passing through judgment."

27. Derrida indicates here the German pagination of *Erfahrung und Urteil*; *Experience and Judgment*, 88. Since the book had not been translated into French at the time, Derrida provides his own translation.

in the perceived object can persist. The object continues to be examined; it continues to be given in such a way that it can be further examined. However, instead of the fulfilment of the intentions of anticipation, a *disappointment* enters in."[28] Husserl gives the following example: Suppose a ball is perceived as uniformly red.[29] Perception gives, and constitutes, from the currently perceived meanings, anticipatory intentions.

That is, I anticipate, based on what I see, what I do not see, and I aim [*viser*] "emptily [*à vide*]" at the hidden part of the ball as also being uniformly red. This is, notice, even before having judged, even before saying "all of the ball is red." At that moment[30] my expectation is disappointed; the back of the ball is not red but green, not smooth but bumpy. I continue to perceive the ball as one and the same ball, and the unity of the intentional process is not compromised. It is still *me* perceiving the *same* ball. But this unity of meaning contains within itself a partial erasure that blurs it to a certain extent. It includes a "not this but that, not like this but rather like that." The red that I anticipated, that I expected, is still a component meaning present in the current perception, but present with an index of "nullity," of "invalidity." This is possible only against the backdrop of temporalization as Husserl describes it, as an intentional dialectic of protention and retention. The *now* is always a tension between, on the one hand, the now that has passed, the one that has just passed and is retained, for if it were not retained we could not perceive the originality of the now, its actuality relative

28. Husserl, *Experience and Judgment*, 88; *Erfahrung und Urteil*, 94.

29. In the interlinear space, there is an addition in parentheses that is most likely: "(on its illuminated side)."

30. In the interlinear space there is an addition: "my perception extending →."

to the past, and, on the other hand, the *now* that is about to arrive, that is anticipated in a protention. Here the sense of the anticipatory expectation of the red is maintained, retained as disappointed expectation, "overcome," says Husserl (*Aufhebung*). The perceived *green* and *bumps* thus also take on a meaning of "polemic" or "contradiction." It is what has *supplanted* the pre-expected quality. (Temporality not in Alain, nor in Bergson.)

This description, though using an example of an external object, could be conducted in an analogous way on any object. It shows, in any case, that "negation is not first the business of the act of predicative judgment but . . . in its original form it already appears in the pre-predicative sphere of receptive experience."[31]

Negation is therefore prior to judgment—affirmative or negative—which allows us to resolve the previous difficulties (Lachelier–Bergson–Goblot conflict). But it is subsequent to doxic certainty, to a kind of original passive affirmation that it does not [illegible word][32] but modifies, which allows us to understand the true meaning of the primacy of the *yes* over the *no*.

Husserl indeed writes that negation is "always a partial crossing-out on the basis of a certitude of belief which is thereby *maintained*, ultimately, on the basis of *the universal belief in the world*."[33]

The results of this Husserlian analysis therefore align with those of Bergson's critique:

1. In that they make no room for a *nothingness*, for any

31. Husserl, *Experience and Judgment*, 90; *Erfahrung und Urteil*, 97.

32. In the manuscript there is an illegible word that might be "endorse [*entérine*]."

33. Husserl, *Experience and Judgment*, 91; *Erfahrung und Urteil*, 98. Derrida's emphasis.

positivity of nothingness, even less for any priority of nothingness;
2. In that they appeal to an experience—here an intentional experience—of disappointment.
But they go beyond Bergson's analysis to the extent that
1. the analysis—I emphasize at the risk of repeating myself—is not psychological;
2. *especially*, the meaning of what is *denied* is *objective*; it is not a subjective illusion. This is because the analysis of subjectivity is much more nuanced and differentiated in Husserl;
3. negative experience (refusal, hatred, indifference [138]).

What does it mean that the meaning of what is *denied*, or of what is *annulled*, *crossed-out*, is *objective*? Let us be clear about this. It is not, of course, in the *real* object (*real* in German), in the red and green ball, which is in fact a full being [*un plein d'être*]. It is therefore not in the world. But it is also not in me, as a real component of my subjectivity, since within me there are only a series of possible noetic acts. But it is in what Husserl calls the *noema*, which is the object as *aimed* at, as it appears to me. Now, this noema is neither (1) the thing itself, in its flesh, and as it exists outside me, in the world, nor (2) a real component of my consciousness since it is an object for my consciousness. *The noema is an intentional and not a real component of consciousness*, says Husserl. Now, remember that the same conflict of the red and green ball *retains*, as a sort of sedimentation, the meaning of disappointment from which it was constituted. The green and the bumps are not the same with or without the disappointment that preceded them. After the disappointment, they are green and bumpy against the backdrop of, against the erasure of, the red and the smoothness that were expected and anticipated. This negativity haunts their meaning and is part of the noema itself. And there is no contradiction here since the noema is *nothing* real insofar as it is a meaning (negativity of meaning and of the object). But this *nothing* has an objective value. And one could reconsider in the light—the recurring light—of this analysis the famous § 49 of the *Ideen*[34] concerning the annihilation of the totality of the world. (I hope we will get to do this by the end of the year.)

When one has followed this Husserlian analysis right to the end, it is difficult to understand the four criticisms that Sartre, in his very brilliant and interesting chapter on "The Origin of Negation" in *Being and Nothingness* (a chapter on which I can offer you only a few insights but which I strongly recommend you read), addresses to Husserl on two points.

(1) Sartre, after initially demonstrating that, clearly, there would be no negation and nonbeing without an *expectation* and a *project* of consciousness (which, by the way, is an axiomatic truth that no philosopher would contest), adds that nonbeings should nevertheless not be reduced to mere subjective phantoms. This is something we have also just seen. Sartre, however, treats Husserl's noema as a phantom of this kind and accuses Husserl in some sense of committing the Bergsonian sin. Here is what he writes (p. 41): "It would be in vain to deny that negation appears on the original basis of a relation of man to the world. The world does not disclose its nonbeings to one who has not first posited them as possibilities. But is this to say that these nonbeings are to be reduced to pure subjectivity? Does this mean to say that we

34. Edmund Husserl, "Absolute Consciousness as Residuum after the Nullifying of the World," in *Ideas: General Introduction to Pure Phenomenology*, trans. W. R. Boyce Gibson (London: George Allen & Unwin Ltd, 1931), 150–53; "La conscience absolue comme résidu de l'anéantissement du monde," in *Idées directrices pour une phénoménologie et une philosophie phénoménologique pures* (Paris: Gallimard, 1950), 160–64.

ought to give them the importance and the type of existence of the Stoic 'lecton,' of Husserl's noema? We think not."[35] Sartre therefore does not take into account Husserl's insistence on pointing out that the noema does not really belong to consciousness.[36]

Then (2) Sartre suspects Husserl of a "thing-illusion" (his expression, p. 63). This thing-illusion would consist of treating the "empty" or "full" intention we have described as something like a *recipient* (empty or full). He says: "Intentions are of psychic nature [it is he, not Husserl, who is speaking erroneously here in the language of psychology] and it would be an error to envisage them in the mode of things, that is, as recipients which would first be given, which according to circumstances could be emptied or filled, and which would be by nature indifferent to their state of being empty or filled. It seems that Husserl has not always escaped this thing-illusion [*illusion chosiste*].[37]

Now, it should go without saying that nothing is more foreign to Husserl than this intention-container. Intention is, for him, an *act* and not a container (for one should, of course, never forget that intentionality is, first, a Husserlian obsession and the denunciation of "contents"), and it undergoes an act, that is, a *noesis*, that *never exists* before or without its objective and noematic correlate.[38]

That said, Sartre provides the most nuanced descriptions of the origin of negation. He insists a great deal and very

35. Jean-Paul Sartre, *Being and Nothingness*, trans. Hazel E. Barnes (New York: Pocket Books, 1968), 38; Jean-Paul Sartre, *L'être et le néant* (Paris: Gallimard, 1953), 41–42.

36. In the manuscript, Derrida here adds: "nonbeing, neither in the world nor in consciousness, in relation, *transition*. (Sartre says this elsewhere)."

37. Sartre, *Being and Nothingness*, 62; *L'être et le néant*, 63.

38. In the manuscript there is a mark indicating an addition: "↔."

concretely on the prejudicative nature of all negative expression and on the nonjudicative origin of negation (without citing *Erfahrung und Urteil*, which was not known in France at the time, I believe . . .). He also shows that it is "on the basis of a pre-interrogative familiarity with being [that] I expect from this being a revelation of its being or of its way of being. The reply will be a *yes* or a *no*."[39]

Thus, the interrogative and hence negative attitude is not necessarily in a situation of interrogative dialogue. I can just as well question my broken-down engine, expect a response from the spark plug, the carburetor, etc.

Nonbeing, if it is thus related to an interrogative project, does not exist *in itself*. Being in itself never admits nothingness within it. It is absolutely full and indestructible. Destruction and fragility, for example, always come to being through man; they are projected significations, without being negative illusions. The same is true for any absence whose perception is constituted by a double nihilation: (1) nihilation of a *background* [fond] and of the world as a whole to perceive the form of a determined absence (Pierre absent in this café)[40]; (2) nihilation of the *form* (the form of the expected and late Pierre who is a nothingness in the fullness of the café and the world). (Read p. 45?)

Nothingness is therefore not in being; it is also not a thing of being. Its mode of being is a *haunting*, presence-absence; nothingness must haunt being for negation to be possible.

39. Sartre, *Being and Nothingness*, 35; *L'être et le néant*, 39. Derrida's emphasis. In the manuscript, after the quotation, Derrida adds and underlines the word "doxa."

40. This example is given by Sartre in section II, "Negations," of chapter 1, "The Origin of Negation," in part II, "The Problem of Nothingness," in *Being and Nothingness*, 40–42; "Les négations," in *L'être et le néant*, 44–45.

But since nothingness is not, that is, is not in itself, it is *nihilated*, it "is-been" [*est été*], says Sartre,[41] by the for-itself. One must then ask what the for-itself must be for the nihilation of the totality of the world to be possible by it. Unfortunately, we do not have time here to pursue this question with Sartre. This power of nihilation defines the for-itself as freedom, and it is in anguish—the anguish that Sartre describes while following and reconciling Kierkegaard and Heidegger—(and here too we would have to ask a few questions of Sartre), and it is in anguish, "the reflexive apprehension of freedom by itself,"[42] that I apprehend myself both as completely free (since I constitute the world in its entirety by surpassing it through my power of nihilation) and as (I quote) "not being able to derive the meaning of the world except as coming from myself."[43] Anguish from which the question "why is there something rather than nothing" can arise;[44] anguish that I cannot escape because the project of escape assumes that I confront this anguish at the very moment I am fleeing from it. This is called "bad faith," a notion Sartre examines in the following chapter.

Let us note, to conclude, that Heidegger was mentioned in passing and integrated—after some criticisms and tweaks—into Sartre's discourse. But it is likely that Heidegger, going just by "Was ist Metaphysik?" (one of his early positions on the matter—and I also recommend reading this very short and dense text, Corbin translation, 1938[45]), would have

41. *Being and Nothingness*, 57; Barnes translates "est été" by "is made-to-be"; *L'être et le Néant*, 58.

42. Sartre, *Being and Nothingness*, 78; *L'être et le néant*, 77.

43. *Ibid.*

44. Derrida here paraphrases Sartre, who is interpreting Heidegger in *Being and Nothingness*, 50–53; *L'être et le néant*, 53.

45. Martin Heidegger, *Was ist Metaphysik?* (Frankfurt am Main: Vittorio Klostermann, 2006); *Qu'est-ce que la métaphysique?*, trans. Henri

rejected this analysis, and Husserl's as well, in fact. The reason is this, and I am simply going to state the principle here. Despite all the progress made in Husserlian and Sartrean analyses over earlier analyses of the origin of negation and "nothingness," these analyses ultimately situate this origin in the project or intentionality of a being called consciousness, transcendental ego for Husserl, for-itself and freedom for Sartre. But a being among others, a type of being among others—even if it is a subject or for-itself—cannot be responsible for the nihilation of the totality of being since, by hypothesis, it excludes itself from that. The most comprehensive phenomenological reduction, the most extensive, the deepest anguish are always in this case inadequate to nihilate the totality of the world, the totality of beings, the totality of regions of being, including man, the for-itself, consciousness.[46] Therefore, one must go beyond this opposition of consciousness-world, for-itself-in-itself, which is too marked by the traditional subject-object opposition, to understand nothingness as the nihilation of the totality of beings. Nihilation of the totality of beings [illegible word][47] on the basis of which the being of beings can appear and the question "why is there being rather than nothing" can arise. Let us note why Heideggerian anxiety [*angoisse*] cannot be Sartre's and perhaps also why Heidegger abandoned this notion because it refers still too much to the human or

Corbin (Paris: Gallimard, 1938); "What Is Metaphysics?," trans. David Farrell Krell, in *Pathmarks*, ed. William McNeill (New York: Cambridge University Press, 1998), 82–96.

46. In the interlinear space there is an added word that might be "region."

47. In the manuscript, there are two illegible words, one of which may be "being [*étant*]." Added in the interlinear space, their exact position is uncertain. They seem to appear after the first word of the sentence, namely, after "nihilation."

to consciousness, guardian of being and sentinel of nothingness (cf. here Heideggerian vigilance and Alain's vigilance).

To which Husserl and Sartre would undoubtedly respond that the transcendental subject and the for-itself are not beings because they are not in the world as objects.[48] Of course. That is also why Heidegger increasingly refuses to start either from being or beings but, rather, from the "*difference* between being and beings," what he calls the ontico-ontological *difference*. This difference[49] through which being shows itself by withdrawing into beings—that is what, at the end of our long but too short journey, which was, rather, a regression, that is what would allow us truly to understand Alain when he says that "to think is to say no."

48. In the interlinear space the following is added: "Region but privileged region—*misunderstanding* = no negation [*point de négation*]."

49. In the interlinear space the following is added: "difference: [an illegible word that might be "link"] and nothingness of negation."

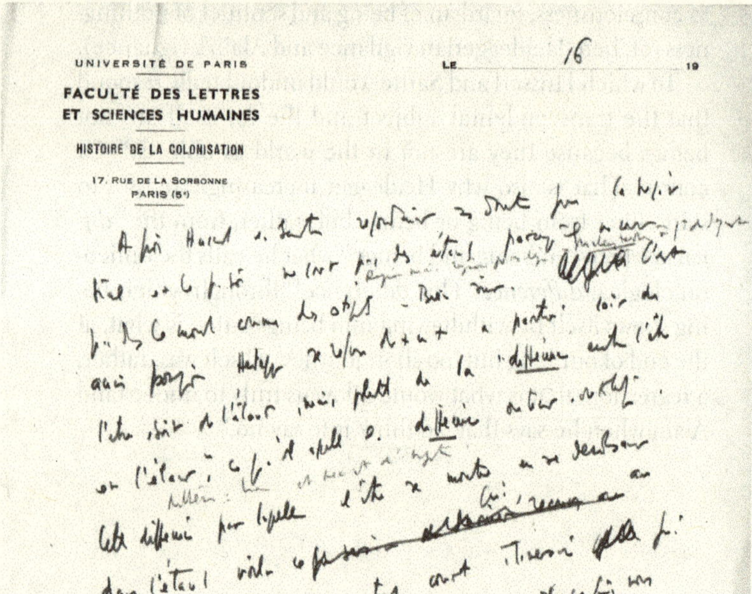

UNIVERSITÉ DE PARIS

FACULTÉ DES LETTRES
ET SCIENCES HUMAINES

HISTOIRE DE LA COLONISATION

17, RUE DE LA SORBONNE
PARIS (5e)

LE 16 19

Paris, I.A.C.

[74]

Figure 5. The final page of Derrida's handwritten manuscript.

Appendix

Sheet 1

Why Sartrean anguish cannot be "metaphysical" (ontology in general)
Cf. the end of *Being and Nothingness.* ontology—metaphysics[1]

1. The order of the pages presented here follows the organization of the Derrida collection of the Critical Theory Archive at the University of California, Irvine. An attempt has been made to transcribe Derrida's notes as closely as possible to the way they appear on the original pages.

Sheet 2

Recall:

1. Describing the level of the pre-predicative allows for an understanding of the experience of negation as hate-aversion-fear-etc. (affect) cf. Heidegger and Sartre.

2. The originality of the meaning of the negated (red ball) arises when discussing judgment.

3. Explain the necessity of the concealment of being to appear in a region.

Sheet 3 (front/back)

Descartes: Nothingness and Defect (Discourse IV)
"I could believe that I derived them [these ideas] from nothingness, that is to say, that they were within me due to what I lacked."

Pascal (*On the Geometric Spirit*, p. 181)
"There are those who claim . . . that two voids of extension can make an extension just as well as two units, none of which are numbers, make a number by their assembly; they should be told . . . that a thousand houses make a city, even though none are cities . . . though a house is not a city, it is nevertheless not a nothingness of a city; there is a significant difference between not being a thing and being a nothingness."

Sartre "Nothingness is not . . . it is nihilated by a being that supports it."[2]
"Man is the being through whom nothingness comes to the world."[3]

2. Derrida here paraphrases Sartre in *Being and Nothingness*, 57; *L'être et le néant*, 58.

3. Sartre, *Being and Nothingness*, 59; *L'être et le néant*, 60.

Sheet 4 (front/back)

Bossuet	on the positivity of negative force: *Logic*: unhappy ≠ not happy Unjust ≠ not just
Sigwart	the idea of negation is defined neither by the presence of a positive mental content nor by its absence. To think of A as absent is to first think of it and thus have it present in the mind.
Kant	no negative concept from a logical point of view. but reality from a transcendental point of view.
Hamilton	"There is no negation conceivable without the concomitant conception of an affirmation: for we cannot deny a thing to exist, without having a notion of the existence which is denied."[4]
Kant	*Critique of Pure Reason*. "From the point of view of our knowledge in general . . . the peculiar function of negative propositions is simply to prevent

4. William Hamilton, *Lectures on Metaphysics and Logic*, 3:216.

error."[5] Quoted by Sigwart, quoted by Bergson.

Lachelier agrees with Goblot's critique (on a logical level) p. 166–167[6]
we can reverse Sigwart's formulation. "This table is white" implies that you could believe it is not.

and *against Bergson*: "If the mind and thought are something and if *existing* means being posited by the mind, the mind can, with the same freedom, posit any being or refuse to posit anything (or at least conceive itself by abstraction as positing nothing, conceiving its own freedom outside of any actual exercise of this freedom). Mr. Bergson's remark is particularly profound and perfectly accurate from the perspective of his realism; but it turns against that very realism. The idea of nothingness implies and verifies the idea of 'freedom' (in my sense of term and not in his)."[7]

5. Derrida here seems to be quoting Henri Bergson, who is himself quoting Kant, in *Creative Evolution*, 287n1 [*L'évolution créatrice*, 312n3]: "Kant, *Critique of Pure Reason*, 2nd ed., 737: 'From the point of view of our knowledge in general . . . the peculiar function of negative propositions is simply to prevent error.' Cf. Christian Sigwart, *Logik*, 2nd ed., vol. 1, 150 ff."

6. E. Goblot, *Traité de logique*, 166–67.

7. J. Lachelier, "Annotations au vocabulaire de la Société française de philosophie," 197–98. Derrida's emphasis.

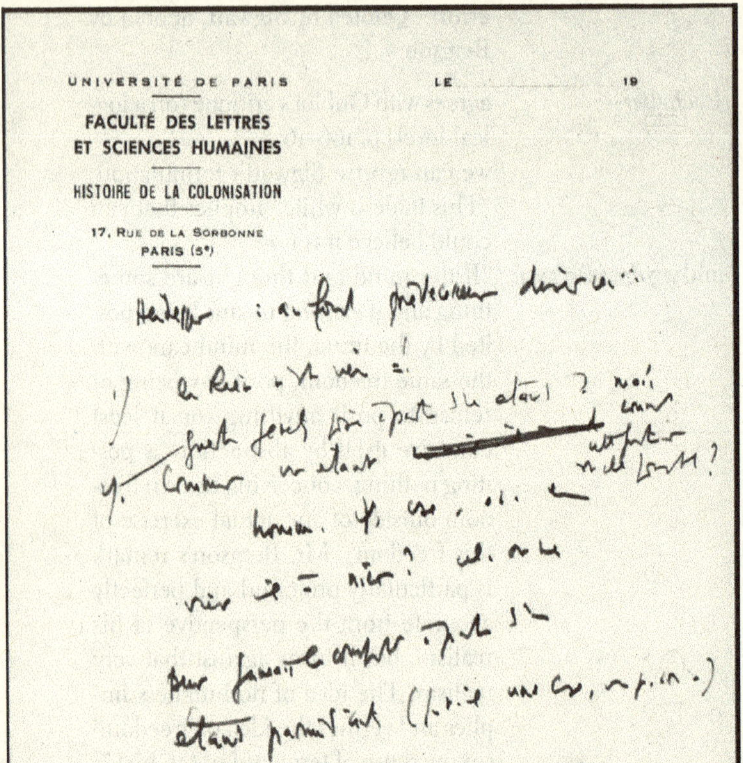
UNIVERSITÉ DE PARIS LE 19

FACULTÉ DES LETTRES
ET SCIENCES HUMAINES

HISTOIRE DE LA COLONISATION

17, RUE DE LA SORBONNE
PARIS (5e)

Paris, I.A.C.

[5]

Figure 6. Handwritten notes corresponding to Sheet 5.

Sheet 5 (front)

Heidegger: fundamentally a predecessor [illegible word]:
(1) the Nothing is nothing = !
(2) Generally, the question is posed from the perspective of beings? But how is this question possible? How does a being, human, philosophy, consciousness, etc., come to deny? This can never be understood on the basis of one being among others (even if it is consciousness, a for-itself); what must be understood is that to think a being in general, one must think the possibility of the non-being [*du non-étant*]. Thus, the question of non-being [*du non-être*] in general to the question. It is through this question that being is announced.

Levinas

Sheet 6 (front)

Do not forget, with Sartre, the prejudicative experience of negation
hatred—etc.

Sheet 7 (front)

—Origin of negation,
Background [in English in original—Trans.] of modern questioning.
Kant: serious consideration of the negative.
Hegel: labor of the negative.
(Before Plato
  = negation = determination
  nonbeing—Descartes
  = privation)[8]

Origin: without going back down below logic
- —*Bergson* (Lachelier) *psychological genesis* without critique
- —Husserl *transcendental genesis* without psychologism
- —Sartre (constitutive negativity[9] of consciousness, priority of the "in-itself").

Conclusion: The *Nothing* is *nothing*. Starting point.

8. From the beginning of this page up to this point, Derrida crosses out his notes.

9. In the interlinear space, the following words are added: "but negation 'prior' to judgment."

Reversal: Heideggerian anxiety [*angoisse*].
the nonbeing [*le non-étant*].[10]

Temporality and negation.

10. Here, "nonbeing [*non-étant*]" is preceded by "nonbeing of beings [*non-être de l'étant*]," which is crossed out.

Sheet 8 (front)

Whether, for Alain, the no does not rest on a more fundamental yes, *meaning*?
—the *axiological yes* .

foundation?[11]
—*nihil privativum et negativum.*
origin of negation.
—ontological yes.

11. An arrow connects "foundation?" to "ontological yes."

Sheet 9 (front)

2nd part:

The yes as the foundation of all negation.

at the level of philosophy ≠ doubt.

negativity of Plat[onic] ideas

no will → nothingness *evil* Plato—Malebranche—Saint Augustine

—skepticism

—Descartes Kant?

—nihilism?

—Lagneau

3rd part: if *yes* seems to be original, where does the no arise? and what does it mean?

—Bergson

—Sartre

—Husserl

—Goblot

—Heidegger

—Birault

Sheet 10 (front)

Alain
Here is my dogma:
To doubt, one must be sure. p. 280[12]
"There would not even be theology without a grain of doubt. 'It is good,' said some doctor, 'that there are heretics.' This is a way of saying that the spirit which no longer knows how to doubt falls below the spirit. And even the virtue of a saint, what else is it but a heroic doubt concerning virtue?"[13]

12. Alain, *Philosophie: Textes choisis pour les classes*, 1:280.
13. Ibid., 283.

Sheet 11 (front)

(3)

—Faith = voluntary belief (as opposed to credulity (p. 250)).[14]

"Those who refuse to believe are men of faith."[15]

—The madman is a person who values all the thoughts that come to him equally (p. 258).[16]

—The madman is a person who believes himself (p. 259).[17]

—Mechanical thought (lying down) p. 260–262[18]

—*One must first believe (yes)* p. 260[19]

Reason and thought

—"There is no consciousness that does not presuppose a world that has always been and will always be."[20]

14. Ibid., 250.
15. Ibid., 260.
16. Ibid., 258.
17. Ibid., 259.
18. Ibid., 260–62.
19. Ibid., 260.
20. Ibid., 26.

Sheet 12 (front)

—Immanence ≠ dualism of body and mind
Braque
—Faith.
After faith.
Double critique
1—to say no presupposes yes.
2—dualism. belief judgment *immanence*
mind-nature
mind-body

Sheet 13 (front)

Belief and faith *in Kant*.

Sheet 14 (front)

No
1. Alain.

2. Negativity and *skepsis*. method (path)
—skepticism.
—doubt.
—*épochè*. ?
existential refusals
freedom

3. Negation

Sheet 15 (front)

Alain Doubt is the salt of the mind.[21]
The function of thinking cannot be delegated.[22]

21. Ibid., 277.
22. Ibid., 277–78.

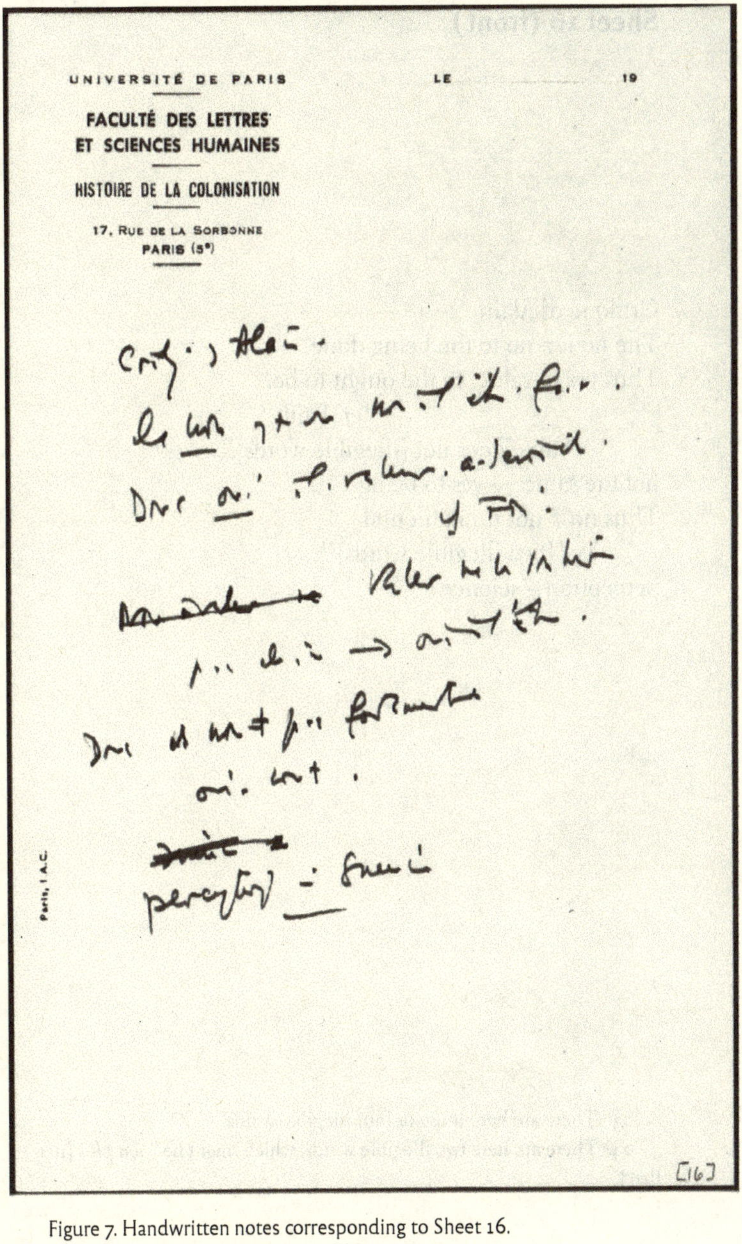

UNIVERSITÉ DE PARIS   LE 19

FACULTÉ DES LETTRES
ET SCIENCES HUMAINES

HISTOIRE DE LA COLONISATION

17, RUE DE LA SORBONNE
PARIS (5e)

Paris, I A.C.

[16]

Figure 7. Handwritten notes corresponding to Sheet 16.

Sheet 16 (front)

Critique of Alain.
The no is a no to the being-done.
Thus *yes* to value, to the ought-to-be.
cf. Faith.
Value does not [illegible words][23]
not the same → yes to being.
Thus no ≠ not fundamental
yes [two illegible words][24]
perception—science

23. There are here three or four illegible words.

24. There are here two illegible words, which might be "*non plus* [neither]."

Sheet 17 (front)

2

Thinking.

"*Thinking means weighing what comes to mind, suspending judgment, controlling oneself, and not indulging oneself.* Thinking is moving from one idea to everything related to it and everything opposed to it in such a way as to align all thoughts with the current thought. *It is thus a rejection of natural thought, and, fundamentally, a rejection of nature, which indeed does not judge thoughts. Therefore, thinking is to judge that not everything in us is as it appears*; it is a long process and a prior peace."[25]

"The incredulous mind is the mind *tout court*" (p. 250).[26]

25. Alain, *Philosophie*, 1:258. Derrida's emphasis.
26. Ibid., 250.

Sheet 18 (front)

—Thinking is saying *yes* = Lagneau
—atheism and [two illegible words][27]
—acquiescence and sleep
—*Cf.* Valéry Sartre
Husserl Bergson

27. In the manuscript there are two illegible words. The first is likely a Greek word. The second might be "inspiration" and is connected by an arrow to "Lagneau."

Sheet 19 (front)

Belief and Truth

"In short, I say that the mind has not yet done anything; but it is that it is not yet awake. We venerate a heap of enormous stones, and true believers add another stone each day. Such is the tomb of Descartes.

One should dare; one does not dare. But do we really know? The doctrine of free judgment is deeply buried. *I see hardly anything but believers. They do have this scruple of believing only what is true. But what one believes is never true.*"[28]

and everything that follows . . . p. 274

Cf. also p. 277

28. Alain, *Philosophie*, 1:273. Derrida's emphasis.

Translators' Acknowledgments

We would like to express our deep thanks to our friends and colleagues of the Derrida Seminar Translation Project (DSTP) for their inestimable help with this translation: Geoffrey Bennington, Ellen Burt, Peggy Kamuf, Kir Kuiken, Elizabeth Rottenberg, and David Wills, as well as the doctoral students who joined the DSTP team in July 2025 at the Institut Mémoires de l'Édition Contemporaine (IMEC) in Caen, Normandy, to help review our translation: Victoria Cheff, Andrew Clark, Scholastique Iradukunda, Bram Nealon, Michael Portal, Rose Taury, and Asena Ulus. Our heartfelt thanks go as well to all the members of the IMEC staff, and in particular François Bordes, for their help, hospitality, and warm welcome during our stay. Finally, we would like to thank Brieuc Gérard, an "alumnus" of DSTP, whose vision, intelligence, and exemplary diligence are responsible for the French edition of this work, and who kindly helped us to prepare this English translation.

Index

This name index records the occurrences of the names of people who appear exclusively in Jacques Derrida's text (including appendices). It therefore excludes the preface as well as the footnotes that consist solely of bibliographic references or those added by the editor.

Jacques Derrida (1930–2004) was one of the most influential philosophers of the late twentieth century. His many books include *Of Grammatology*, *Specters of Marx*, and *The Animal That Therefore I Am*.

Brieuc Gérard is an independent scholar based in Los Angeles.

Pascale-Anne Brault is Professor of French at DePaul University. She is the translator of fifteen books by Jacques Derrida, Barbara Cassin, and others and is Director of the Derrida Library series at Editions du Seuil.

Michael Naas is Professor of Philosophy at DePaul University. His most recent book is *Threshold Phenomena: Derrida and the Question of Hospitality* (2024). He is the translator of twelve books by Jacques Derrida, Jean-François Lyotard, and Jean-Luc Nancy.